Teach Yourself Italian: © 2016 by Yeral E. Ogando
Publisher: Christian Translation LLC
Printed in the USA
Cover Design by SAL media

All rights reserved. No part of this publication may be reproduced, stored in a retrieval system, or transmitted in any form or by any means—now known or hereafter—such as electronic, mechanical, photocopy, recording or otherwise—without the prior written permission of both the copyright owner and the publisher. The only exception is brief quotations in printed reviews.

This is a work of fiction. Names, characters, dialogue, places, and incidents are either a product of the author's imagination and are used fictitiously. Character's opinions are not necessarily the same as the authors. Any resemblance to persons living or dead is purely coincidental; they are not to be interpreted as real people or events.

ISBN 13: 978-0-996687355
ISBN 10: 0996687351

1. Language Learning 2. Italian Language

DEDICATION:

This book is dedicated to the Unique and forever-lasting person who has always been there for me, no matter how stubborn I am:
GOD

I also want to dedicate this work to YOU (the reader), because you have taken the moment to read this incredible story and without you I would not have been here.

You all have a special place in my heart.
Always.

ACKNOWLEDGMENTS:

Gratitude to my Lord God for giving me the opportunity to write this book; Teach Yourself Italian, dedicated to God above all, then to my daughters Yeiris & Tiffany, my beloved father Ubersindo, my lovely grandparents Seferina and Rey Luis. To my friend Aneudys Peguero and Marco Stagi, who were my guide and pillars for me to learn this language, without them, this book would not be possible.

I also want to dedicate this work to all of you, who wants to succeed in life and special to Nicoletta Natoli, who has revised the contents of this book and helped me creating the final edition.

This book has been inspired by all of you, thus providing you with an easy and comphensive tool to learn the language quickly.

Teach Yourself Italian

I encourage you to study the content of this book and you will see positive results in short time.

God bless you all

Dio vi benedica

Dr. Yeral E. Ogando

www.aprendeis.com

Acknowledgements

Introduction

- Alphabet and rules of pronunciation
- Remarks and Special combinations
- Pronunciation Chart
- Expressions

UNIT 1

Buongiorno – Good Morning

Grammar

- Personal Pronouns
- Simple Present
    - Essere - To be

Teach Yourself Italian

- **Question Words**

    - Chi – Who

    - **Dove - Where**

Gender of names and Adjectives

- Masculine

    - Singular

    - Plural

- Feminine

    - Singular

    - Plural

- Gender's chart - Masculine and Feminine

Review Exercises

- Vocabulary

- I giorni della settimana – Days of the week
- I mesi dell'anno – Months of the year
- Le stagioni dell'anno - Seasons of the year
- Temperature's Phrases

UNIT 2

Sí, Ce l'ho – Yes, I have it.

Grammar

- Simple Present
  - Avere - To have
- Question words

  - Che cosa / Quale – What

  - C'è – There is

  - Ci sono - There are

- Prepositions

Teach Yourself Italian

- Sul / Sulla -   On

- Nel / Nella - In

Review Exercises

Vocabulary

- Emergenza - Emergency

- Viaggi - Trips

UNIT 3

All'università - At the University

Grammar

- Simple Present
    - First Group -Are
    - List of verbs from the first group
    - Special Attention to Verbs in -Iare

- Second Group -Ere

    - List of verbs from the Second group

- Third Group -Ire

- - List of verbs from the Third group
- Verbs with the suffix ISC
  - List of verbs with ISC Suffix
- Definite Article
  - Masculine
  - Feminine
- Definite Article's Chart - Masculine and Feminine
- Indefinite Article
  - Masculine
  - Feminine

Indefinite Article's Chart - Masculine and Feminine

Review Exercises

Vocabulary:

Dogana - Customs

Teach Yourself Italian
UNIT 4

Tanti Auguri – Happy Birthday

Grammar

- Possessive Adjectives

    o **Masculine**

    o **Feminine**

- Question word

    o Di chi – Whose

- Four irregular verbs from the first group in present tense

    o Andare - To go

    o Stare - To be

    o Fare – To do – to make

    o Dare – To give

Main irregular verbs and its conjugations

Present Progressive or -ING form of the verbs

Review Exercises

UNIT 5

Al Bar – At the Bar

Grammar

- Simple Past or Present Perfect Simple
  - Verbs that take the auxiliary Essere in the Simple Past or Present Perfect Simple form.
  - Verbs that take the auxiliary Avere in the Simple Past or Present Perfect Simple form
  - **Some irregular verbs in the past participle**

Common adverbial expressions often used with this time.

Teach Yourself Italian

Chart of combinations of Prepositions with articles

Aggettivi - Adjectives

Review Exercises

- Vocabulary
    - Auto – car
    - Il Treno – the train
    - La nave – Ship
    - L'aeroplano – Airplane
    - Taxi

UNIT 6

Sento Nostalgia – I am homesick

Grammar

- Simple Future

    - **Verbs from the first (-are) and second group (-ere) take the same ending.**

    - **Verbs from the third group (-ire) take the following endings:**

- Irregular verbs in the future

    - **Verbs that end in ciare (cominciare – start - begin) to make the future.**

    - **Verbs that end in giare (mangiare - eat) to make the future.**

    - **Verbs that end in care (dimenticare - forget) to make the future.**

    - **Verbs that end in gare (pagare - pay) to make the future.**

Simple Perfect

Teach Yourself Italian

Perfect Future

Review Exercises

- Vocabulary:
    - Main prepositions
    - I numeri cardinali – Cardinal Numbers
    - I numeri ordinali – Ordinal Numbers
    - Le quattro Operazioni – Math Operations
    - Segni di punteggiatura – Punctuation Marks.

UNIT 7

La Serata – The Night Out

Grammar

Reflexive Pronouns

Simple Past reflexive

Review Exercise

- Vocabulary:
    - Cinema
    - Teatro – Theater
    - Museo - Museum

UNIT 8

Le Donne hanno la precedenza – Ladies first

- Grammar
    - Direct Object Pronouns
    - Strong Direct Pronouns
    - Partitive Pronoun "ne"
    - The particle CI plus the prenominal particles MI, TI, VI
    - Particle CI plus pronouns LO, LA, LI, LE, NE
    - CI sono – There are with the partitive particle "ne"
- Vocabulary:
    - Chiesa - Church

Teach Yourself Italian
UNIT 9

Non La Sopporto – I can't stand her

- Grammar
    - Direct pronouns in past tense
    - LO, LA, LI, LE plus the verb in past participle
    - MI, TI CI, VI, LA plus the verb in Simple Past or Present Perfect Simple
    - Partitive pronoun "ne" plus the verb in Simple Past or Present Perfect Simple
- Vocabulary
    - Albergo – Hotel
    - Ristorante - Restaurant
    - Menù - Menu

UNIT 10

Voglia di Uscire – Would you like to go out?

- Grammar
    - Imperfect Time – Past
    - First Group   - Are
    - Second Group - Ere
    - Third Group – Ire

- Verbs Essere and Avere in the imperfect time
- Past Perfect
- Preterit Perfect

Review Exercises

- Vocabulary:
    - Banca – Bank
    - Feste – Holidays
    - Corrispondenza - Mail
    - Affari – Business
    - Telefono / Posta – Telephone/Post Office

UNIT 11

Cosa Vorresti Fare? – What would you like to do?

- Grammar
    - Present Conditional
    - First Group -Are and Second Group -Ere
    - For the Third Group -Ire
    - Present Perfect Conditional

Review Exercises

- Vocabulary

Teach Yourself Italian
- Caffetteria – Cafeteria / Cafe
- Bar – Bar
- Birreria – Beer Pub
- Visite - Visits

UNIT 12

Macchina in Prestito – A borrowed car

- Grammar
  - Indirect Object Pronouns

Review Exercises
- Vocabulary
  - Famiglia - Family

UNIT 13

Un Ladro – A Thief

- Grammar
  - Prepositional Articles
- Vocabulary
  - Persone di Servizio – Housekeeping Staff
  - Oggetti - Objects

UNIT 14

Non Mi Faccia Male – Don't hurt me

- Grammar
    - Imperative with Lei and Loro
    - Verbs from the -Ere and -Ire groups
    - Pay special attention to the verbs in the third group (-Ire) that take the suffix Isc
    - Imperative and Pronouns

Review Exercises
- Vocabulary:
    - Circolazione – Traffic
    - Casa – House
    - La scuola - School

UNIT 15

Sulla Spiaggia – On the Beach

- Grammar
    - Imperative with Tu-Noi-Voi
    - Some irregular verbs in the imperative tense
    - Special Cases

Teach Yourself Italian

- Dare – Give
- Dire – Say / Tell
- Fare – Do / Make
- Andarsene – Go away / Leave

- Vocabulary
- Signs - Segnali/Avvisi

UNIT 16

Che Numero Porta? – What's your size?

- Grammar
    - Relative Pronouns
    - Chi, Che, Cui, and Il quale

Review Exercises

- Vocabulary:
    - L'abbigliamento – Clothing
    - Farmacia – Drugstore
    - Medico – Doctor
    - Malattie – Diseases
    - Sintomi - Symptoms

- Italian Joke - Dal barbiere

UNIT 17

Una Bella Ragazza – A beautiful girl

- Grammar
    - Present Subjunctive Tense
    - Phrases that call for the subjunctive tense
    - Present Perfect Subjunctive
    - Irregular verbs in the Subjunctive

Review Exercises
- Vocabulary:
    - Sport
    - Pesca – Fishing
    - Tennis
    - Animali - Animals

UNIT 18

Un Capolavoro – A Masterpiece

- Grammar
    - Past Perfect Subjunctive
- Vocabulary:
    - L`ora – The time
    - Corpo Umano – Human Body
    - Convenevoli – Greetings
    - Frasi - Phrases

UNIT 19

Me ne vado – I am leaving

Teach Yourself Italian

- Grammar
  - Hypothetical Period

Review Exercise

- Vocabulary
  - Mestieri e Professioni – Crafts and Professions
  - Espressioni – Expressions
  - Esclamazione - Exclamations

UNIT 20

Ricchi Sfondati – Filthy Rich

- Grammar
  - Italian Adjectives
  - Positive Adjectives
  - Comparative
    - Di Maggioranza – Majority
    - Di minoranza – Minority
  - Relative Superlative
  - Absolute Superlative
  - Irregular Comparatives and Superlatives
  - Avverbi – Adverbs

- Gli Avverbi di luogo che rispondono alla domanda Dove - Adverbs of place answering to Where
- Avverbi Affermativi-Negativi-Dubitativi - Affirmative – Negative and Doubt Adverbs
- Avverbi di quantità – Adverbs of quantity
- Avverbi di luogo più comuni – More common adverbs of place

Review Exercises

UNIT 21

Niente di nuovo - Nothing new

- Grammar
    - The Remote Past Tense
    - Verbs of the first Group -Are
    - Verbs of the second group -Ere
    - For third group verbs -Ire

Teach Yourself Italian

- Irregular verbs in the Past Remote Tense
  - Essere – Be
  - Fare – Do / Make
  - Dire – Say / Tell
  - Bere – Drink
  - Dare – Give
  - Stare - Be
- Irregular verbs in the First, Third person of the singular and Third person of the plural

- Preterit Perfect Tense

- Avverbi di tempo – Adverbs of time

Review Exercises

UNIT 22

La Guida Racconta – The travel guide says

- Grammar
  - Active Tense
  - Passive Tense

Review Exercises
- Vocabulary:
  - Congiunzioni – Conjunctions

Conclusion

Biography

Glossary of Verbs

Glossary of Words

Bonus Page

Teach Yourself Italian

Introduction

I have published this method for you to learn this language in a very quick and comprehensive way.

I kindly ask you to take 20 minutes of your time on a daily basis without interruption, so you can concentrate and digest the content of this work.

One of the biggest challenge in learning is to be a Self-Taught person, in other words, learn by yourself, it requires lots of discipline and dedication in your study. To study a full hour every day would make you feel tired and bored very quickly, that's why I recommend to you a minimum of 20 minutes per day and a maximum of 40 minutes per day, therefore, you will be achieving better results.

I wish you good luck in this amazing trip to the world of learning, and remember "Be shameless to speak".

Dr. Yeral E. Ogando

www.aprendeis.com

Teach Yourself Italian

Before starting

You may think that it will be difficult to learn Italian, but you will be surprised when you realize how quick you can learn to recognize the words and language. To learn with this method, you will need to follow systematically the lessons on this course, taking special interest in each one of our lessons, thus giving you the basis for a better learning experience.

Make sure to have the MP3 Audio Handy, because you will need it to practice the correct pronunciation of the words. Italian Language has a few sounds that may sound new to your ears, but if you listen very carefully and repeat the words clearly, you will be soon pronouncing the words correctly. I recommend you to always read out loud, so you hear yourself and compare your pronunciation with the one in the MP3 Audio. Remember to always consult the pronunciation guide.

Do not forget, it is more productive and effective to study 20 minutes per day, instead of dedicating long hours at a time. Your concentration will be best profited when taking 20 minutes a day.

I've divided the alphabet into 21 letters as you see below.

Alphabet and rules of pronunciation

Teach Yourself Italian

The following consonants *B – D – F – G – L – M – N – P – S – T - V* are pronounced as in English.

A *(ah)*

Examples: Acqua – Water   Armonia - Harmony

B

Examples: Bene - Fine - Good – Well

Birra - Beer

C   *(chi)*

Followed by "e-i" sounds like "CH" in English:

Examples: Cena - Dinner

Cibo   -   Meal - Food

Followed by other vowels it is pronounced like in English:

    Examples: Cosa - Thing   Casa - House

Followed by "He-Hi" is pronounced like "ke - ki" in English:

    Examples: Che - What   Chi - Who

D

Examples: Dio – God   Dialetto - Dialect

*See pronunciation's chart

E   *(e)*

It is pronounced as in Edward.

Examples: Eccitante – Exciting

Esame - Exam

Teach Yourself Italian

F

Examples: Facile – Easy   Fede - Faith

*See pronunciation's chart

G

Followed by "e-i" has the English sound of the letter J:

> Examples: Gente - People
>
> Gigante - Giant

Followed by "He-Hi" has the English sound as in **Ge**t and **Gui**-tar:

Examples: Spag**he**tti - Spaghetti

Ghiotto   - Glutton

Followed by other vowels it sounds like in English, but when it is followed by "Li", the "g" becomes silent leaving just the L sound.

Examples: Migliaio - Million

Taglio (talio) - Cut

H *(ac-ca)*

It is always silent, never pronounced.

Examples: Hotel   - Hotel

I *(e)*

It is pronounced as I in the English word India.

Examples: Insalata – Salad

Istruttore - Instructor

L

Examples: Lavoro – Work / Job

　　　　Ladro - Thief

Teach Yourself Italian

*See pronunciation's chart

M

Examples: Mercato – Market

Melone Melon

*See pronunciation's chart

N

Examples: Naso – Nose

Natura - Nature

*See pronunciation's chart

O   *(oh)*

It is pronounced like the O on Oscar.

Examples: Odore – Smell   Oggi - Today

P

Examples: Paese – Country   Pane - Bread

*See pronunciation's chart

Q *(cooh)*

It is always followed by the vowel U and it is pronounced like in Quest, always pronouncing the

U.

Examples: Questo - This

Quando - When

R   *(ehrr)*

It is pronounced a little stronger than the English R.

Teach Yourself Italian

Examples: Reale – Real   Regole - Rule

S

When it is not a doubled S, it is pronounced softer than the English S, more like the French S, but when it is doubled, it is then pronounced like a regular English.

> Examples: Casa - House
> Cassa - Box

When it is before a consonant, it sounds just as in English.
Examples:
Studente - Student   Scuola - School

T

Examples: Tavolo – Table

Tasca - Pocket

*See pronunciation's chart

U   *(ooh)*

It is pronounced everywhere you see it and it sounds like the doubled oo in Pooh.

Examples: Guerra - War
Guida - Guide

V

It sounds just as in English.

Examples: Vacca - Cow   Vegetale - Vegetable

Z *(dzehta)*.

Teach Yourself Italian

When it is doubled and in between vowels it is pronounced as TS:

>Examples: Pazzo   -   Crazy
>
>Pizza - Pizza.

When it is single, not doubled, it is pronounced Z, but softer:

Examples : Zaino   -   School Bag

Zucchero - Sugar

Remarks and Special combinations:

GN

It is a foreign sound to the English speaking student, it can be found in French and in the Spanish Ñ:

Examples: Montagna - Mountain

Spagnolo - Spanish

Sce - Sci

This is a very special combination in the Italian language, equivalent to the English SH:

Examples: Scena   - Scene

Scemo - Dumb / Idiot

Very Important: All the consonants in Italian can be doubled with the exception of H and Q, which makes the doubled sound when adding a C before it.

Examples: *Acqua* - *Water*

Teach Yourself Italian

There's an exception with all the words from the family of Soqquadro – Mess / Disorder

All the doubled consonants are pronounced. To pronounce a double consonant, just make a little pause on the first one and it will give you the doubled sound. Please note that making the difference in pronunciation is a must, because it can change the meaning of the words.

Examples:

Camino - Chimney   Cammino - Path / Way

Pena - Sorrow   Penna - Pen

Caro - Dear   Carro - Cart

Capello - Hair   Cappello - Hat

Pala - Shovel   Palla - Ball

Casa - House   Cassa - Box

Seno - Breast Senno - Sense / Good Judgment

Note - Notes   Notte - Night

Cane - Dog   Canne - Canes

Sete - Thirst   Sette - Seven

Remember,

To make the distinction between a single consonant and a doubled consonant, make a little pause and stress the doubled consonant to get the native sound. Make sure to listen very carefully to the native pronunciation in the Audio and you will soon master the sound.

Study and master this pronunciation chart with all the combinations you will find in Italian. Once you master it, you will be able to read anything in Italian. Pay close attention to the

Teach Yourself Italian
native pronunciation and practice it until you

master it.

Pronunciation Chart

Ba	*Be*		*Bi*		*Bo*	*Bu*
Ca	*Che*		*Chi*		*Co*	*Cu*
	Ce		*Ci*			
Da	*De*		*Di*		*Do*	*Du*
Fa	*Fe*		*Fi*		*Fo*	*Fu*
Ga	*Ghe*		*Ghi*		*Go*	*Gu*
	Ge		*Gi*			
La	*Le*		*Li*		*Lo*	*Lu*
Ma	*Me*		*Mi*		*Mo*	*Mu*
Na	*Ne*		*Ni*		*No*	*Nu*
Gna	*Gne*		*Gni*		*Gno*	*Gnu*
Pa	*Pe*		*Pi*		*Po*	*Pu*

Teach Yourself Italian

Ra	Re	Ri	Ro	Ru
Sa	Se	Si	So	Su
Ta	Te	Ti	To	Tu
Va	Ve	Vi	Vo	Vu
Za	Ze	Zi	Zo	Zu
Scia	Scie		Scio	Sciu
Sce				

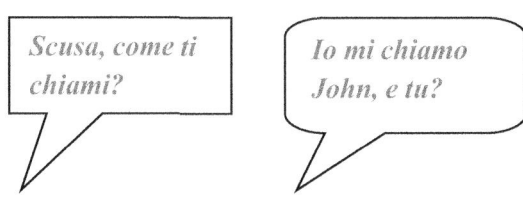

Scusa, come ti chiami?

Io mi chiamo John, e tu?

Expressions

Italiano

Buongiorno — Good morning

Sì — Yes

No - No

Ciao - Hello – Hi – Goodbye (when leaving)

Mi piace - I like it

Per favore - Please

Aiutatemi - Help me

Grazie - Thanks

Mi scusi - Excuse me

Ci vediamo - See you

Come ti chiami? - What's your name?

Come si chiama? - What is your name? (Polite)

Mi chiamo - My name is

Il suo nome è? - Your name is? (polite)

Come stai? - How are you?

Come sta? - How are you? (polite)

Molto bene - Very well

Teach Yourself Italian

Bene, grazie - Well, thanks

Piacere - Pleased to meet you

Il suo indirizzo è? - Your address is? (polite)

Il mio indirizzo è - My address is

Quanto costa? - How much does it cost?

Il mio telefono è - My phone number is

Dov'è il bagno? - Where is the rest room (bathroom)?

Per Uomini - For men

Per Donne - For women

Mi dispiace - I am sorry

Congratulations

You are now ready to read in Italian, you are ready to start with the first lesson. Do not forget to review the words you've already learned in Italian, read them out loud and write them as well. Review the pronunciation with the MP3 audio if you are not certain about any pronunciation. Then read the words in English and try to see if you can remember the meaning in Italian. Do not worry if you cannot remember them all at first. "Practice makes perfect."

Teach Yourself Italian
UNIT 1

Buon giorno – Good Morning

In this Unit you will learn:

- ❖ To speak in the present tense, using personal pronouns and asking questions with the verb To Be.
- ❖ To use the Gender of things, how to use singular and plural;
- ❖ Several useful terms such as: days of the week, months and seasons of the year and temperature's phrases.

Buongiorno

Marco: Buongiorno ragazzo, scusami, **sei** tedesco?
Daniel: Sì, **sono** tedesco, di Amburgo. E lei, signore, **è** straniero?
Marco: No, io **sono** italiano. Perché **sei** in Italia?

Daniel: Sono in Italia per imparare la lingua italiana.
Marco: Sei uno studente?
Daniel: Sì, e **sono** in Italia in vacanza-studio. Ah, io mi chiamo Daniel. E lei, signore, come si chiama?
Marco: Io mi chiamo Marco. Piacere! Arrivederci Daniel e buona vacanza!
Daniel: Arrivederla signore!

Buon – Good
Giorno – day
Ragazzo - boy
Scusami – Excuse me
Tedesco - German
Sì - Yes
Di - From
Amburgo - Hamburg
E – and
Lei – You (polite)
Signore - Sir / Mr

Italia - Italy
Per – for / to
Imparare – to learn
La lingua – the language
Uno studente – a student
Vacanza – Holiday / Vacation
Studio - Study
Io - I
Mi chiamo – My name is

Teach Yourself Italian

Straniero - foreigner
Italiano - Italian
Perché – Why
Piacere – My pleasure / nice to meet you
Arrivederci – Goodbye
Buona vacanza – enjoy your vacation
Arrivederla – Goodbye (polite or for a female speaker)

Come Si chiama – What is your name (polite)

Grammar

Personal Pronouns

Io   I

Tu   You

Lui/Lei   He - She

Lei   You (polite)

Plural – Plurale

Noi   We

Question Words
Chi – Who

Chi è Pietro? Lui è un ragazzo italiano

Who is Pietro? He is an Italian boy

Teach Yourself Italian

Chi sono Daniel e Pietro?   Loro sono dei ragazzi tedeschi

Who are Daniel and Pietro? They are German boys

Dove - Where

Dov'è la ragazza?   La ragazza è a casa

Where is the girl?   The girl is at home

Dove sono le ragazze? Le ragazze sono a casa

Where are the girls? The girls are at home

Gender of names and Adjectives

There are only two Genders in Italian, masculine and feminine

Masculine

Almost all the words end in **O**, some in **E** and very few in **A**.

Singular	*Plural*

O   Nonno – Grandfather   Nonni - Grandfathers / Grandparents

E   Cane - Dog   Cani - Dogs

A   Pianeta - Planet   Pianeti - Planets

For all the masculine words, the plural is formed by substituting the last vowel with *i.* In other words, they all make the plural by changing the last vowel for i.

You could say that every word ending in O is masculine, with a few exceptions that you will see below.

Teach Yourself Italian

Feminine

Almost all feminine words end in **A** and a few in **E.**

Singular   *Plural*

A   Finestra - Window   Finestre - Windows

E   Chiave - Key   Chiavi - Keys

It means that all the words in Italian make their plural by substituting the last vowel with the vowel "i", except the feminine words ending in "A", which make their plural by substituting final A for "E".

In Italian there are no words ending in consonant, those you'll find are borrowed words from another language.

There are only six words ending in O from the feminine Gender: *Mano (hand) Radio – Auto – Moto – Dinamo (dynamo) - Eco.*

Gender's chart Masculine and Feminine

Masculine		Feminine	
Singular	*Plural*	*Singular*	*Plural*
O	I	*A*	*E*
E	I	E	I
A	I		

Teach Yourself Italian

Review Exercises

1. **Answer with the correct form of the verb Essere**

a) Chi è Daniela? (ragazza italiana) - *Daniela è una ragazza italiana*

b) Chi è Pietro? (ragazzo tedesco) - _____

c) Chi sono Daniela e Pietro? (ragazzi americani) - _____

d) Chi sono Daniela e Nicoletta? (ragazze turche) - _____

Remarks. In Italian every name must match gender and number.

2. **Answer with the correct pronoun and form of Essere in affirmative.**

a) (Lei) è straniero? – *Sí, io sono straniero.*

b) (Lei) è americana? -

_____

c) (Tu) sei polacco? -

_____

d) (Voi) siete spagnoli? -

_____

3. Complete with the correct form of Essere in negative.

a) Io _ ___ tedesco, ma turco. *Io **non sono** tedesco, **ma** turco.*

b) Tu _ ___ americano, ma italiano.

_____

c) Noi _ ___ americani, ma tedeschi.

_____

d) Voi _ ___ greche, ma turche.

_____

*Remarks: **Non** is used to construct the negative part of a sentence.*
      ***Ma**, literally means but.*

4. Transform singular into plural.

Teach Yourself Italian

a) La ragazza è seduta. *Le ragazze sono sedute.*

b) Il signore è straniero.
   _____

c) La signora è americana.
   _____

d) Il ragazzo è italiano.
   _____

5. Put the plural to these words:

a) Posto------------Parete----------Ragazzo-------- ----Straniero----------

b) Bambino---------Signore---------Treno--------- -------Lavoro------------

c) Libro------------ Tavolo----------Quaderno---- -------Caso---------------

d) Tetto------------ Dente------------Dolore---------- ---- Asino--------------

e) Ragazza------------Casa---------------Mensa----------

f) Straniera----------Volta-------------- Lingua------------Vacanza-------------

Vocabulary:

I giorni della settimana – Days of the week

Lunedì - Monday

Martedì - Tuesday

Mercoledì - Wednesday

Giovedì - Thursday

Venerdì - Friday

Sabato - Saturday

Domenica - Sunday

I mesi dell'anno – Months of the year

Gennaio - January   Luglio - July

Febbraio - February Agosto - August

Marzo - March   Settembre - September

Aprile - April   Ottobre - October

Teach Yourself Italian

Maggio - May   Novembre - November

Giugno - June   Dicembre - December

Le stagioni dell'anno - Seasons of the year

Primavera - Spring   Estate - Summer

Autunno - Fall / Autumn   Inverno - Winter

Temperature's Phrases

Che giorno è oggi - What day is today

Oggi è lunedì, primo Gennaio - Today is Monday, January the 1st

In che stagione siamo? - What season are we at?

Siamo in inverno - We are in summer

È una bella giornata - It is a beautiful day

Sta piovendo - It is raining

Fa caldo - It is hot / warm

Fa freddo - It is cold

C'è vento - It is windy

Sta nevicando - It is snowing

La temperatura è mite / tropicale - The temperature is warm - tropical

Il cielo è limpido - Sky is clear

Non pioverà - It is not going to rain

Il cielo è buio - Sky is dark / cloudy

Forse pioverà - Maybe it will rain

Ci vediamo domenica prossima - See you next Sunday

Sarò lì fra poco - I will be there shortly

Teach Yourself Italian
UNIT 2

Sì, ce l'ho – Yes, I have it.

In this Unit you will learn:

- ❖ To speak in present tense using the verb to have and asking questions.
- ❖ To use There is and There are, the prepositions In and On.
- ❖ Emergency and trips vocabulary.

Sì, ce l'ho

La segretaria: Tu sei Daniel Schwarz?
Lo studente: Sì, sono qui per frequentare un corso di italiano.
La segretaria: Hai un documento?
Lo studente: Sì, ho tutto. Ecco il passaporto, le fotografie...
La segretaria: Hai anche un numero di cellulare?
Lo studente: No, perché non ho il telefono.
La segretaria: Grazie, lei è molto gentile.

Lo studente: Prego!

Qui – here
Frequentare – Attend - Assist
Un corso di Italiano – an Italian course
Un documento – a document
Tutto – everything - all
Ecco il passaporto – here you have the passport
Le fotografie - pictures
Anche – also - too
Numero di cellulare – cellphone number
Non – used to create negative sentences
Il telefono – the telephone

Grammar

Simple Present

Avere - to Have

Io ho Pazienza - I am patient

Tu hai Dubbi - You have doubts – you're doubtful

Teach Yourself Italian

Lui/lei ha La certezza - He / She is certain - sure

Lei ha Fortuna - You (polite) are lucky

Noi abbiamo Denaro - We have money

Voi avete Paura   - You (pl) are afraid

Loro hanno Soldi - They have money

Question words

Che – What

Che cosa è?   È una matita

What is it (this)?   It's a pencil

Che cosa sono?   Sono (delle) matite

What are these (they)? These are pencils

C'è – There is   Ci sono - There are

C'è un ragazzo in chiesa   - There is a boy at the church

Ci sono dei ragazzi in Chiesa - There are some boys at the church

Prepositions

On -   Sul / Sulla

Cosa c'è sul banco?   C'è una chiave

What's on the bench?   There's a key

Che cosa c'è sulla sedia?   Ci sono dei fogli

What's on the chair? There are some papers

Teach Yourself Italian

In - Nel / Nella

Che cosa c'è nel cassetto?   Non c'è niente

What's in the drawer? There is nothing

Cosa c'è nella borsa? Ci sono delle chiavi

What's in the purse? There are some keys

Review Exercises

1. **Answer with the correct form of Avere.**

   a) Lei ha un libro? – ***Sì, io ho un libro.***

   b) Voi avete la macchina? -
   _____

   Negative Answers

c) Hai un fiammifero? – *No, non ho un fiammifero.*

d) Hai un foglio? -

 _____

2. Answer with the correct form using Sul – Sulla, Nel – Nella, C'è, Ci sono.

   a) Dove è il giornale? (Sul banco) - *Il giornale è sul banco.*

   b) Dove è la borsa? (Sulla sedia) -

   _____

   c) Dove sono le chiavi? (Nella borsa) -

   _____

   d) Dove sono i fogli? (Nel cassetto) -

   _____

   e) Che cosa c'è sulla sedia? (i libri)- **Sulla sedia ci sono i libri.**

   f) Che cosa c'è sul banco? (una borsa) -

   _____

g) Che cosa c'è nella borsa? (i libri) - _____

Vocabulary

Emergenza - Emergency

Aiuto sono straniero - Help me please, I am foreigner

Dov'è la centrale di polizia - Where is the police station

Chiami la polizia - Call the police

Devo denunciare un furto - I must report a robbery

Mi hanno rubato tutto - They have robbed me everything

Ho perso il Passaporto - I've lost the passport

Ho avuto un incidente - I've had an accident

La macchina deve essere trainata - The car must be towed

Subito un'ambulanza - Hurry-up, call an ambulance

Dove si trova l'ospedale - Where is the hospital

La clinica più vicina - The closest clinic

È una chiamata urgente - It is an urgent call

C'è del fumo nella casa - There's smoke in the house

Chiami i pompieri - Call the firefighters

È una emergenza - It is an emergency

Viaggi - Trips

Teach Yourself Italian

Dov'è l'agenzia di viaggi? - Where is the travel agency?

Può darmi un biglietto aereo? - Can you give me a flight ticket?

Quanto costa il biglietto di andata e ritorno? - How much is the roundtrip?

Avete una carta della città? - Do you have a city map?

Si, ce l'abbiamo - Yes, we do.

Dov'è l'aeroporto? - Where is the airport?

Quanto dista? - How far is…?

A che ora parte l'autobus? - What times does the bus leave?

Facchino mi porta il mio bagaglio, per favore? - Porter, can you carry my luggage, please?

Quando arriva l'aereo? - What time does the plane arrive?

UNIT 3

All'università - *At the University*

In this unit you will learn how:

- ❖ To conjugate the verbs in simple present, use the articles, possessive pronouns
- ❖ To use Irregular verbs in present tense and gerund
- ❖ To use the definite and indefinite articles and vocabulary about customs.

All'università

Daniel: Buongiorno professore!
Professore: Buongiorno... Aspetta!... tu sei Daniel, Daniel Schwarz. Come **stai**?
Daniel: Bene, grazie. Lei come **sta**? **Insegna** ancora nella stessa Università?
Professore: No, non **insegno** più, sono in pensione. E tu che fai? **Studi**?
Daniel: Sì, **studio** all'Università, **frequento** il primo anno di legge.
Professore: Allora **studi** molto!

Teach Yourself Italian

Daniel: È vero, professore, **esco** raramente. Invece di **uscire** con gli amici, preferisco **studiare** o **leggere** un libro.

Professore: Bravo, sono contento di **sentire** queste cose. Hai il mio numero di cellulare?

Daniel: Sì, ce l'ho.

Professore: Bene, così ci **sentiamo** presto. Chiamami!

Daniel: Certamente professore, a presto.

Professore: Ciao ciao, Daniel.

Professore – Professor
Aspetta - Wait
Come stai – How are you
Bene - Fine
Grazie – Thanks
Come sta – How are you (polite)
Insegnare – To teach
Ancora – Still / Yet
Stessa - Same
Università - University
Più – More
In pensione – Retired
Che fai – What do you do
Studiare – To study
Il primo – The first

Anno - Year
Legge - Law
Allora - So
Molto – Much / Very
È vero – It is true
Raramente - Rarely
Invece – Instead of
Uscire – To go out
Con – With
Gli amici - Friends
Preferire – To prefer
Leggere – To read
Un libro – A book
Bravo – Congratulations
Contento – Glad / Happy
Sentire – To feel (referring to emotions) / To hear (referring to hearing)
Il mio - My
Così - Like this
Ci sentiamo - We'll talk (literally, we will hear)
Presto - Soon
Chiamami – Call me
Certamente – Certainly
A presto – See you soon

Teach Yourself Italian

Grammar

Simple Present: conjugation of the three groups in present tense.

First group of verbs ends in -ARE, this is the pattern to conjugate all regular verbs from this group in the present tense.

All the verbs from this group are regular with an exception of four verbs that we will see later on.

ARE:

Parl**are** - To speak / talk

Io	Parl-**o**	- I speak
Tu	Parl-**i**	- You speak
Lui/lei	Parl-**a**	- He / She speaks
Lei	Parl-**a**	- You speak (Polite)

Noi	Parl-**iamo**	- We speak
Voi	Parl-**ate**	- You speak (plural)
Loro	Parl-**ano**	- They speak

Remarks:

To conjugate the verbs, you just need to strike out the ARE ending and then add the correct conjugation for each pronoun.

It is very important to note that when pronouncing the conjugation for Loro P*a*rlano, the accent falls in the first A, therefore, you need to stress the first A in P*a*rlano.

List of verbs from the first group.

Cantare - To sing

Ascoltare – To listen

Studiare - To study

Teach Yourself Italian

Trovare - To find

Amare - To love

Ricordare – To remember

Fumare - To smoke

Insegnare – To teach

Saltare - To jump

Frequentare – To attend / to assist

Lavare - To wash

Passare – To pass

Lavorare – To work

Arrivare – To arrive

Aspettare – To wait

Viaggiare – To travel

Guardare – To watch / to see

Preparare – To prepare

Salutare - To greet

Abitare - To live / to dwell

Domandare – To ask

Sognare – To dream

Cacciare - To hunt

Indicare – To indicate

*Mangiare – to eat

*Sbagliare – To make a mistake

*Marciare – To march

*Lasciare - To leave

*Espiare - To spy

**Pagare – To pay

*Rinviare – To resend

Teach Yourself Italian

*Rimediare – To remedy / to cure / to heal

*Cambiare – To change

*Accorciare – To shorten

Cavalcare – To gallop

*Avviare – To start up a plane

**Navigare – To navigate

*Cominciare – To start

Prorogare – To prorogue / to extend

Stracciare – To tear / to rip up

**Caricare   - To carry / To load / To charge

**Sporcare   - To dirty

Verbs ending in -Iare.

When conjugating these verbs that end in -IARE, you do not double the I in the second person.

Example:

Tu mangi – you eat

Tu cominci – you start

Tu sbagli – you are wrong

***Pay close attention to these verbs from the first group in the **Tu - you** and **Noi - we** form*

Caricare	*Pagare*	*Navigare*	*porcare*
Carico	Pago	Navigo	Sporco
Cari**ch**i	Pa**gh**i	Navi**gh**i	Spor**ch**i
Carica	Paga	Naviga	Sporca
Carica	Paga	Naviga	Sporca

Teach Yourself Italian

Cari**chi**amo	Pa**ghi**amo	Navi**ghi**amo	Spor**chi**amo
Caricate	Pagate	Navigate	Sporcate
Cari**c**ano	Pa**g**ano	Navi**g**ano	Spor**c**ano

The pattern for this four verbs will serve you for other verbs like them. Pay special attention to the pronunciation on the conjugation for Loro – They.

Second group of verbs ends in -ERE, this is the pattern to conjugate all regular verbs from this group in the present tense.

-ERE:

Scriv**ere** - To write

Io   scriv-**o**   I write

Tu	scriv-**i**	You write
Lui/lei	scriv-**e**	He / She writes
Lei	scriv-**e**	You write (polite)
Noi	scriv-**iamo**	We write
Voi	scriv-**ete**	You write (plural)
Loro	scriv-**ono**	They write

List of verbs from the Second group

Leggere - to read

Rispondere – to answer – to respond

Ricevere - to receive

Pretendere – to pretend

Prendere - to take

Stendere – to lay – to spread

Chiedere – to ask

Teach Yourself Italian

Correre – to run

Mettere – to put

Conoscere – to know

Vivere – to live

Comprendere – to understand

Chiudere – to close

Cadere – to fall

Ridere – to laugh

Decidere – to decide

Third group of verbs ends in -IRE, this is the pattern to conjugate all regular verbs from this group in the present tense.

-IRE:

Dormire - to sleep

Io	Dorm-**o**	I sleep
Tu	Dorm-**i**	You sleep
Lui/lei	Dorm-**e**	He / She sleeps
Lei	Dorm-**e**	You sleep (polite)
Noi	Dorm-**iamo**	We sleep
Voi	Dorm-**ite**	You sleep (plural)
Loro	Dorm-**ono**	They sleep

List of verbs from the Third group

Partire – to leave – to depart

Coprire – to cover

Sentire – to feel – to hear

Offrire – to offer

Aprire – to open

Teach Yourself Italian

Scoprire – to discover

Bollire – to boil

Verbs with the suffix ISC

There are some verbs from this group that take the prefix **"ISC" in the first, second and third person of the singular** *(Io – I, Tu – You, Lui / lei – He / She, Lei – You polite)* and in the third person of the plural *(Loro - They)*.

Finire – to finish – to end

Io Finisco

Tu Finisci

Lui/lei Finisce

Lei Finisce

Noi Finiamo

Voi Finite

Loro Finiscono

Verbs with ISC Suffix

Spedire - to send

Capire – to understand

Preferire - to prefer

Definite Article

Masculine

Il – it is used in front of words that start with consonants and its plural is I

Il globo - the sphere   I globi - spheres

Teach Yourself Italian

Lo is used with words that start with S, *Z, GN, PS and its plural is* Gli.

Lo studente – the student   Gli studenti - students

Lo gnomo – the dwarf   Gli gnomi - dwarfs

Lo zaino - the school bag   Gli zaini - school bags

L' is used in front of words that start with vowels and its plural is Gli

L'occhio – the eye   Gli occhi - eyes

Feminine

The article La is used in front of words that start with a consonant, and its plural is Le.

La casa – the house   Le case – houses

L' is used in front of words that start with a vowel, and its plural is Le.

L'aiuola - the flowerbed   Le aiuole - flowerbeds

Definite Article's Chart - Masculine and Feminine

Masculine		*Feminine*	
Singular	*Plural*	*Singular*	*Plural*
Il	I	La	Le
Lo	Gli	L'	Le

Teach Yourself Italian

L'	Gli

Indefinite Article

Masculine

<u>Un</u> - is used in front of words that start with vowels and consonants, and its plurals are Dei and Degli.

Un libro - a book   Dei libri - some books

Un angelo – an angel   Degli angeli – some angels

Before words that start with a vowel, you must use degli for the plural.

<u>Uno</u> - it is used in front of words that start with S, Z, GN, PS, and its plural is Degli.

Uno Studente – a student   Degli studenti – some students

Feminine

<u>Una</u> - it is used in front of words that start with a consonant and its plural is Delle.

Una sarta - a tailor Delle sarte – some tailors

<u>Un'</u> - it is used in front of words that start with vowels and its plural is Delle.

Un'erba - a herb Delle erbe – some herbs

Indefinite Article's chart - Masculine and Feminine

	Masculine		*Feminine*	
Singular	Plural	Singular	Plural	

Teach Yourself Italian

Un	Dei - Degli	Una	Delle
Uno	Degli	Un'	Delle

Review Exercises

1. Answer with the correct form of the verb.

   a) Cosa aspetti? (l'autobus) – *Aspetto l'autobus.*

   b) Cosa aspettate? (la lezione del professore) - _____

   c) Cosa fa Pietro? (guardare la televisione) - _____

   d) Che cosa bevete? (una birra) - _____

   e) Cosa capisci? (tutto) - _____

   *Remarks: If you are asked with **Voi** (you plural), your answer must be with **Noi** (we).*

   As you could have seen most of the time, the pronouns are not necessary, because the conjugation of the verbs tells you what person you are referring to.

2. **Complete by asking the correct question.**

   a) ***Chi prepara la tesi***   ?
      Pietro prepara la tesi.

   b) _____ ?
      Leggiamo il giornale.

   c) _____ ?   Vado al cinema.

   d) _____ ?   Lavoro in ospedale

   e) _____ ?   Studio all'università.

3. **Answer the following questions in affirmative and negative sentences.**

   a) Puoi rispondere a questa domanda?

      + Sì, ***posso rispondere a questa domanda.***

Teach Yourself Italian

- Mi dispiace, *ma non posso rispondere a questa domanda.*

b) Puoi rimanere ancora?

+ Sì,

_____

- Mi dispiace,

_____

c) Potete venire oggi?

+ Sì,

_____

- Mi dispiace,

_____

d) Potete scendere subito?

+ Sì,

_____

- Mi dispiace,

_____

Vocabulary:

Dogana - Customs

Sono qui per turismo - I am here on a tourist trip

Per affari - Business trip

Non ho nulla da dichiarare - I have nothing to declare

Solo effetti personali - Only personal items

Avete qualcosa da dichiarare? - Do you have something to declare?

Apra la valigia per favore - Open your luggage, please

Teach Yourself Italian

Quanto denaro avete? - How much money do you carry?

Va bene, potete andare - It is ok, you can go

Riempia questo modulo - Fill out this form

UNIT 4

Tanti Auguri – Happy Birthday

In this Unit you will learn:

- ❖ To use possessive adjectives, male and female, singular and plural.
- ❖ To use main irregular verbs in the present tense.
- ❖ To understand the difference between Essere and Stare.
- ❖ To use the present progressive or ING of the verbs.

Tanti Auguri

Daniel: Pronto! Pietro, sono Daniel. Senti, puoi venire oggi a casa mia? Voglio organizzare una festa per il mio compleanno.
Pietro: Va bene, vengo da te verso mezzogiorno.
Daniel: D'accordo. Ci vediamo dopo.
------ (Pietro arriva da Daniel)-------
Pietro: Chi pensi di invitare?

Teach Yourself Italian

Daniel: Tutti i nostri compagni di classe. Facciamo il conto: noi due con i nostri compagni di classe siamo nove, più i miei genitori fa undici.

Pietro: Giancarlo non viene, quindi undici meno uno fa dieci. Compriamo panini e bibite per circa quindici persone.

*(Pietro canta: tanti auguri a te, tanti auguri a te, tanti auguri a **Daniel**, tanti auguri a te).*

Voglio – I want
Organizzare – to organize
Una festa – a party
Compleanno - Birthday
Va bene – It is ok
Da te – At your place. When Da is used it is most of the times referring to the house of the person. It can also means "by, from" depending on the contexts.
Verso - around
Mezzogiorno – midday
D'accordo – Ok / Fine
Ci vediamo dopo – see you later
Invitare – to invite
Compagni di classe – classmates

Facciamo il conto – let us count
Nove - nine
Genitori - parents
Undici - eleven
Quindi - therefore
Dieci - ten
Compriamo – we buy
Panini - breads
Bibite - drinks
Circa – approximately
Quindici – fifteen
Persone – people

Grammar

Possessive Adjectives

Maschile - Masculine		
Singolare	*Plurale*	
Il Mio	I Miei	My - Mine

Teach Yourself Italian

Il Tuo	I Tuoi	Your - Yours
Il Suo	I Suoi	His (Your – Yours / Polite masculine)
Il Nostro	I Nostri	Our - Ours
Il Vostro	I Vostri	Your - Yours (plural)
Loro	Loro	Their - Theirs

Femminile - Feminine		
Singolare	Plurale	
La Mia	Le Mie	My - Mine
La Tua	Le Tue	Your – Yours
La Sua	Le Sue	Her – Hers (Your – Yours / Polite feminine)

La Nostra	Le Nostre	Our - Ours
La Vostra (Plural)	Le Vostre	Your – Yours
Loro	Loro	Their - Theirs

Remarks: with family names in singular the article is not used, but when using the plural form, the articles are used.

Mia nonna – Le mie nonne   My grandmother – My grandmothers

Mio fratello – I Miei fratelli   My brother – My brothers

Question word

Di chi – Whose

Di chi è questo libro? È il suo.

Teach Yourself Italian

Whose is this book? - It is his or it is yours (polite form)

Di chi sono questi libri? Sono i suoi

Whose are these books?   These are his or these are yours (polite form)

These are the four irregular verbs from the first group in present tense:

Andare - to go   ****Stare** - to be

Io Vado *a* New York   Sto

Tu Vai *in* Germania   Stai

Lui/lei Va *da* Pietro   Sta

Lei   Va   Sta

Noi   Andiamo   Stiamo

| Voi | Andate | State |
| Loro | Vanno *in* gelateria | Stanno |

** "Stare" is used with the meaning of to be only in regional variants of Italian. Instead you could use "Trovarsi", Io mi trovo, tu ti trovi, lui si trova, etc.

Fare – to do – to make   **Dare – to give**

Io	Faccio	Do
Tu	Fai	Dai
Lui/lei	Fa	Dà
Lei	Fa	Dà
Noi	Facciamo	Diamo
Voi	Fate	Date
Loro	Fanno	Danno

Teach Yourself Italian

Remarks:

With the infinitive of the verbs and city names the preposition *"a" is used.*

With nations and regions names the preposition *"in" is used.*

With people's names the preposition *"da" is used.*

With names ending in *–eria* the preposition *"in" is used.*

** Difference between Essere and Stare

Essere means to be or to exist, and stare usually means to stay, but it is used with English idiomatic use "to be".

***Essere* indicates more permanent aspects of people or things, for example:**

a) Identity – *Io sono Pietro.* (I am Pietro)

b) Profession – *Lui è un professore.* (He is a teacher)
c) Origin – *Noi siamo della Sicilia.* (We are from Sicily.)
d) Religious or political affiliation – *Io sono cattolico* (I am Catholic)
e) Time of day or date – *Sono le nove.* (It is 9 o'clock.)
f) Possession – *La casa è di Marco.* (It is Marco's house.)
g) Nationality – *Sono italiano.* (I am Italian.)
h) Physical aspects or characteristics of something – *Il tavolo è verde.* (The table is green.)
i) Essential qualities of something or someone – *Lui è vecchio. Tu sei antipatico.* (He is old. You are unpleasant.)
j) Location – *Il tavolo è in cucina.* (The table is in the kitchen.)
k) Condition or emotion that is subject to change – *Sono malato.* ("I am sick.")
l) Personal observations or reactions, how something seems or feels – *La casa è pulita.* (The house is - seems clean.)

Stare indicates precise locations, in idioms and as auxiliary, for example:

a) Idiomatic sentences – *Sto bene.* (I am well.)

Teach Yourself Italian

b) Idiomatic sentences – *Sto male.* (I feel bad.)
c) Location – *La sedia sta (si trova) in cucina.* (The chair is in the kitchen.)
d) Continuous tense – *Sto correndo.* (I am running.)

Main irregular verbs and its conjugations

Volere – want	Sapere – know	Nascere - be born
Io Voglio	So	Nasco
Tu Vuoi	Sai	Nasci
Lui/lei Vuole	Sa	Nasce
Lei Vuole	Sa	Nasce
Noi Vogliamo	Sappiamo	Nasciamo
Voi Volete	Sapete	Nascete
Loro Vogliono	Sanno	Nascono

Volere ragionare con calma — Want to think calmly

Sapere tante cose — Know many things

Uscire – go out	Bere – drink	Morire – die
Esco	Bevo	Muoio
Esci	Bevi	Muori
Esce	Beve	Muore
Esce	Beve	Muore
Usciamo	Beviamo	Moriamo
Uscite	Bevete	Morite
Escono	**Be**vono	Muoiono

Morire di spavento — Frightened to death

Teach Yourself Italian

Scegliere – choose	Salire – go up	Trarre – carry
Scelgo	Salgo	Traggo
Scegli	Sali	Trai
Sceglie	Sale	Trae
Sceglie	Sale	Trae
Scegliamo	Saliamo	Traiamo
Scegliete	Salite	Traete
Scelgono	Salgono	Traggono

Scegliere il momento opportuno To choose the right moment

Dovere - have to	Potere – can	Togliere - remove
Devo (debbo)	Posso	Tolgo
Devi	Puoi	Togli

Deve	Può	Toglie
Deve	Può	Toglie
Dobbiamo	Possiamo	Togliamo
Dovete	Potete	Togliete
Devono (Debbono)	Possono	Tolgono

Devo scappare subito - I must escape quicky – I have to escape quickly

Venire – come	Dire – say / tell	Cogliere – pick up
Vengo	Dico	Colgo
Vieni	Dici	Cogli
Viene	Dice	Coglie
Viene	Dice	Coglie
Veniamo	Diciamo	Cogliamo
Venite	Dite	Cogliete

Teach Yourself Italian

| V**e**ngono | D**i**cono | C**o**lgono |

Cogliere l'occasione - Profit the occasion / Get the chance

Da dove viene? Vengo da Londra - Where do you come from? I come from London

Porre – put	**Tradurre** – translate	**Cucire** - sew
Pongo	Traduco	Cucio
Poni	Traduci	Cuci
Pone	Traduce	Cuce
Pone	Traduce	Cuce
Poniamo	Traduciamo	Cuciamo
Ponete	Traducete	Cucite
P**o**ngono	Trad**u**cono	C**u**ciono

Cucire il vestito   Sew the dress

| **Tenere** – have | **Tacere** – be silent / still |

Tengo	Taccio
Tieni	Taci
Tiene	Tace
Tiene	Tace
Teniamo	Taciamo
Tenete	Tacete
Tengono	Tacciono

Tacere per non sbagliare   Be silent to avoid mistakes

Sciogliere – Unleash	**Cuocere** - cook	**Rimanere** - stay
Sciolgo	Cuocio	Rimango
Sciogli	Cuoci	Rimani
Scioglie	Cuoce	Rimane
Scioglie	Cuoce	Rimane

Teach Yourself Italian

Sciogliamo	C(u)ociamo	Rimaniamo
Sciogliete	C(u)ocete	Rimanete
Sciolgono	Cuociono	Rimangono

Cuocere la verdura   Cook the vegatables

Sciogliere il cane   Unleash the dog

Rimanere all'angolo della strada   Stay at the corner of the street

Piacere – like / love	**Parere** – seem / appear
Piaccio	Paio
Piaci	Pari
Piace	Pare
Piace	Pare
Piacciamo	Paiamo
Piacete	Parete

Piacciono	Paiono

Mi piace mangiare   I like to eat

Present Progressive or -ING form of the verbs

This time is formed using the conjugation of the verb **Stare** plus the verb with an ending, that varies for each group of verbs.

The verbs of the first group -ARE take ANDO

Parlare   Parl**ando - speaking**

Sto parlando con te – I am speaking with you

The verbs of the second and third groups ERE – IRE take ENDO.

Scrivere   Scriv**endo - writing**

Teach Yourself Italian

Dorm**ire**   Dorm**endo** - sleeping

Lui sta scrivendo una lettera - He is writing a letter

Loro stanno dormendo – They are sleeping

Review Exercises

1. **Answer using the correct possessive adjectives**

    a) Questa è la casa di Pietro? *Sì, questa è la sua casa.*

    b) Queste sono le valigie del nipote? _____

    c) Signora, questa è sua figlia? - _____

    d) Professore, queste sono le sue chiavi? _____

    e) Dove è il vostro libro? (nella borsa) _____

    f) Dove sono i miei giornali? (sul tavolo) _____

g) Dove sono i vostri vicini? (in viaggio) _____

2. Complete using the Present Progressive – ING correctly.

a) Mi *sto lavando* i capelli. (Lavare)

b) Alessandra si ____ ____ . (Annoiare)

c) _____ ____ di fumare. (Smettere)

d) I bambini _____ ____ in cortile. (Giocare)

e) Che bello! _____ ____ il Natale. (Arrivare)

f) Scusami se ti _____ ____ . (Disturbare)

g) I bambini _____ ____ . (Crescere)

Teach Yourself Italian

h) Stai _____? (Studiare)

3. *Complete using the correct response to:* Cosa stai facendo? What are you doing?

a) In questo momento *(io, guardare)* la TV.
   *In questo momento io **sto guardando** la TV.*

b) Maria e Marco *(loro, andare)* al cinema.

c) Pietro, tu *(tu, sprecare)* il tuo tempo!

d) Silenzio! Il bambino! *(lui, dormire)*

e) Francesca ed io *(noi, pulire)* il garage.

f) Caro Luca, tu e Michele *(voi, studiare)* molto bene.

g) Marla *(lei, scrivere)* una lunga lettera.

h) **(io, venire)** a casa.

UNIT 5

Al Bar – At the Bar

In this unit you will learn:

- ❖ To use Simple Past or Present Perfect Simple of the verbs in Italian
- ❖ To recognize verbs that take the auxiliary Essere and Avere
- ❖ To use the irregular form of the verbs in this time
- ❖ To deepen your knowledge with the chart of combinations for prepositions and articles
- ❖ To use important adjectives in Italian
- ❖ To learn new words on means of transportation, such as: Car, train, ship, airplane and taxi.

Al Bar

Pietro: Ciao, Daniel, come stai?
Daniel: Sto bene, grazie, e tu?
Pietro: Non c'è male. Bevi qualcosa con me?
Daniel: Volentieri! Prendo una birra.
Pietro: Ieri non sei venuto al bar.

Teach Yourself Italian

Daniel: Sì, non c'ero. Sono tornato a casa stamattina. Ho trascorso una settimana di vacanza in Francia con i miei genitori. E tu che hai fatto in questi giorni?

Pietro: Niente di particolare. Mi sono annoiato. Sono stato spesso in casa da solo, ho ascoltato tanta musica e ho guardato la TV.

Daniel: La mia vacanza invece è stata interessante... abbiamo girato a piedi per Parigi e abbiamo avuto sempre una fame e una sete incredibili!

> Non c'è male – Expression meaning there's no problem
> Qualcosa - something
> Volentieri – Gladly / willingly
> Ieri – yesterday
> Sì, non c'ero – Yes, I was not in.
> Stamattina – This morning
> Niente di particolare – Nothing in particular
> Mi sono annoiato – I got bored
> Spesso – often
> Tanta musica – a lot of music
> Interessante - interesting
> Girato a piedi – walked on foot

Parigi - Paris
Sempre – always
*Fame - Hungry
*Sete – Thirsty
Incredibili – incredible

Remarks:

In Italian you say:

Ho fame – I am hungry, literally, I have hunger.
Ho sete – I am thirsty, literally, I have thirst.

Grammar

Simple Past or Present Perfect Simple

This time is translated in two different ways in English, Simple Past and Present Perfect Simple. It expresses a fact or action that happened in the recent past or that occurred long ago but still has consequences to the present.

Teach Yourself Italian

Ho parlato con te — **I spoke** with you or **I have spoken** with you

In Italian you use the verbs **Essere** and **Avere** as auxiliary verbs to make the past participle. This construction is made with simple present of the verbs **Essere** and **Avere** and the past participle of the verbs.

- ✓ Past participle for the verbs of the first group -ARE is made by changing Are with **ATO**

  Parlare   Parl**ato**

- ✓ Past participle for the verbs of the second group -ERE is made by changing Ere with **UTO**

  Credere   Cred**uto**

- ✓ Past participle for the verbs of the third group -IRE is made by changing Ire with **ITO**

Partire   Part**ito**

For the third group this is the general rule, but there can be a lot of exceptions.

Examples:

Ho mangiato una mela - I ate an apple or I have eaten an apple

Lui ha creduto a te - He believed in you or he has believed in you

Loro hanno parlato di te - They spoke about you or they have spoken about you

Remarks:

Teach Yourself Italian

You will use the Auxiliary Essere when the verbs are related to movements, arriving and departing points. Examples of verbs of actions and movements:

Il treno è partito alle nove - The train left at nine or the train has left at nine
Sono arrivato ieri notte - I arrived yesterday evening

Verbs that take the auxiliary Essere in the *Simple Past or Present Perfect Simple* form.

Venire - come

Succedere - happen

Costare - cost

Entrare – get in / enter

Riuscire – succeed in

Rimanere - stay / remain

Uscire – go out

Diventare - become

Salire – go up

Stare - be

Tornare – return / come back

Scendere – go down

Piacere – like / love

Restare – stay / remain

Nascere – be born

Morire - die

When you use the auxiliary **Essere** the past participle must agree both in gender and number.

Teach Yourself Italian

Maria è andata al cinema - Maria went to the cinema or Maria has gone to the cinema

Carlo è andato in centro - Carlo went downtown or Carlo has gone downtown

Loro sono andati al cinema - They went to the movies or they have gone to the movies

Loro sono andate in centro - They went downtown or they have gone downtown

When you use the auxiliary Avere the past participle remains the same, unchanged.

Avere		Essere
Io	Ho mangiato	Sono Andato (a)

Tu	Hai mangiato	Sei Andato (a)
Lui/lei	Ha mangiato	è Andato (a)
Lei	Ha mangiato	è Andato (a)
Noi	Abbiamo mangiato	Siamo Andati (e)
Voi	Avete mangiato	Siete Andati (e)
Loro	Hanno mangiato	Sono Andati (e)

Verbs that take the auxiliary Avere in the *Simple Past or Present Perfect Simple* form

Comprare - buy

Decidere - decide

Scrivere - write

Mangiare - eat

Chiudere - close

Teach Yourself Italian

Chiedere - ask

Vendere - sell

Fare – do / make

Dire – say / tell

Avere - have

Leggere - read

Trascorrere – spend / elapse / pass

Vedere – see / watch

Prendere - take

Bere - drink

Finire – finish / end

Mettere - put / put in

Aprire - open

Preferire - prefer

Spendere – spend

Scoprire - discover

Some irregular verbs in the past participle

Accendere – Light / Turn on	**Acceso**
Vedere – see / watch	**Visto**
Conoscere – know / meet	**Conosciuto**
Rimanere – stay / remain	**Rimasto**
Scoprire - discover	**Scoperto**
Succedere – happen	**Successo**

Bere - drink	**Bevuto**
Trascorrere – elapse / pass	**Trascorso**
Dire – say / tell	**Detto**

Teach Yourself Italian

Prendere - take	**Preso**
Fare – do / make	**Fatto**
Decidere - decide	**Deciso**
Vivere - live	**Vissuto**
Vincere – conquer / win	**Vinto**
Spendere - spend	**Speso**
Aprire - open	**Aperto**
Scrivere- write	**Scritto**
Scendere – go down	**Sceso**
Rompere – break	**Rotto**
Piangere - cry	**Pianto**
Nascondere - hide	**Nascosto**
Muovere - move	**Mosso**
Mordere - bite	**Morso**

Mettere – put / put in	**Messo**
Leggere - read	**Letto**
Invadere- invade	**Invaso**
Giungere - reach / arrivare	**Giunto**
Friggere - fry	**Fritto**
Dividere- divide	**Diviso**
Dirigere- direct - guide	**Diretto**
Dipingere – paint	**Dipinto**
Correre- run	**Corso**
Chiudere - close	**Chiuso**
Chiedere - ask	**Chiesto**
Essere - be	**Stato**

Common adverbial expressions often used with this time.

Teach Yourself Italian

Ieri - yesterday

Ieri pomeriggio - yesterday afternoon

Ieri sera - last night

Il mese scorso - last month

L'altro giorno - the other day

Stamani - this morning

Tre giorni fa - three days ago

Chart of combinations of Prepositions with articles

M. Singular	M. Plural	F. Singular	F. Plural	M. Singular	M. Plural
Il	I	La	Le	Lo	gli

Combinations

A	Al	Ai	Alla	Alle	Allo	Gli
– to			All'		All'	

Al padre – to the father , allo scolaro – to the student , alla madre - to the mother

ai padri – to the fathers , agli scolari – to the students , alle madri – to the mothers

Da – at	Dal	Dal	Dalla	Dall e	Dallo	Dagli
			Dall'		Dall'	

dal nonno – at grandfather's house , dallo sposo – at the husband's house , dalla zia – at the aunt's house

Teach Yourself Italian

dai giovani – at the (from, By) Young people's house , *dagli ebrei* – at the (from, By) Hebrews' house , *dalle cugine* – at the (from, By) cousins' house.

Di	Del	Dei	Della Dell'	Dell e	Dello Dell'	Degli
of

del cane – of the dog , *dello scolaro* – of the student , *della madre* – of the mother

dei cani – of the dogs, *degli scolari* – of the students , *delle madri* – of the mothers

In	Nel	Nei	Nella Nell'	Nell e	Nello Nell'	Negli
In

nel pozzo – in the well, *nello studio* – in the studio, *nella stanza* – in the room

nei nidi – in the nests, *negli armadi* – in the

closets, nelle casse – in the boxes

S	Sul	Sui	Sulla	Sull	Sullo	Sugl
u			Sull'	e	Sull'	i
–						
O						
n						

sul tavolo – on the table, sullo specchio – on the mirror, sulla nave – on the ship

sui monti – on the mountains, sugli occhi – on the eyes, sulle spalle – on the shoulders

Remarks: CON - with and **PER – for or by**, they are used normally. The use with the prepositions is only found in ancient writings, because it is no longer used.

Con il cane – with the dog

Per le ragazze – for the girls

Teach Yourself Italian

Aggettivi - Adjectives

Alto – high / tall

Aperto - open

Bello – beautiful / handsome

Biondo - blond

Buono - good

Caldo – hot / warm

Caro – dear (when referring to a person) / expensive (when referring to prices)

Divertente - funny

Dritto – straight / right

Veloce – fast / quick

Stanco - tired

Secco - dry

Ricco - rich

Pulito - clean

Nuovo - new

Lungo - long

Leggero - light

Grasso - fat

Largo - wide

Grande - big

Piccolo – small / little

Vecchio - old

Avaro - greedy

Giovane - young

Generoso - kind / generous

Forte - strong

Facile - easy

Duro – hard / tough

Teach Yourself Italian

Dolce - sweet

Lento - slow

Fresco - fresh

Debole - weak

Difficile - difficult

Molle - soft

Amaro - bitter

Storto - twisted

Umido – humid

Povero - poor

Sporco - dirty

Usato - used

Corto - short

Pesante - heavy

Stretto - narrow

Magro – thin / skinny

Basso – low / small

Chiuso - closed

Bagnato - wet

Brutto - ugly

Bruno - brown

Cattivo – bad / evil

Freddo - cold

A buon mercato – cheap (expression)

Noioso - boring

Male – bad / wrong

Review Exercises

1. **Complete with the correct form of the verb in past participle.**

Teach Yourself Italian

a. Che cosa hai comprato? (dei souvenir). *Ho comprato dei souvenir.*

b. Con chi hai passeggiato? (con Daniel) _____

c. Che cosa avete ordinato? (un cappuccino) _____

d. Che cosa avete deciso? (di rimanere qui) _____

e. Dove sei andato? (a Firenze)
_____

f. Con chi sei uscita? (con Pietro)
_____

g. Dove sei stata? (a cena fuori)
_____

h. A che ora sei partito? (alle 7)
_____

2. **Fill in the blank with the correct form for the verb in past participle.**

   a) A che ora sei-------- (arrivare) ieri sera?
   A che ora sei arrivato ieri sera?

b) Quando siete------ (partire)?

c) Io sono-------- (uscire) alle 9:00

d) Lui è-------- (diventare) un bravo ragazzo

e) Lei ha-------- (credere) a me

f) Tu hai------ (prendere) soldi in prestito

3. **Transform these sentences into their plural form**

   a) Lei è stata a Roma--- ***Loro sono state a Roma***

   b) Io ho mangiato l'uovo—
   _____

   c) L'amico ha ricevuto un vaglia—
   _____

   d) Il ragno è uscito dal buco—
   _____

   e) Il mendicante ha avuto il pane—
   _____

Vocabulary

Teach Yourself Italian

Auto - car

Vorrei affittare un'auto   - I would like to rent a car

Sono nella strada giusta per - Am I at the right street for…

Il pieno, normale   - Full tank, regular

Vi prego venitemi a prendere - I beg you to come and pick me up

Può mandarmi un meccanico? - Can you send me a mechanic? / You can send me a mechanic

Quanto tempo occorre? - How long does it take to?

L'autobus   - The bus

L'autista   - The driver

L'autocarro - The truck

Il camioncino - The little truck

Il porta bagagli - The trunk

Il Treno – the train

La locomotiva - The locomotive

La carrozza - The carriage

Il vagone - The wagon

La sala d'aspetto - Waiting room

Il capotreno - Train conductor

Il controllore - Ticket inspector

Il macchinista - Train Driver

La stazione - The station

Il deposito bagagli - Luggage room

Teach Yourself Italian
La nave - Ship

Motonave	Motor vessel
Vaporetto	Steamer
Nave a vela	Sailing ship
Barca	Boat
Canoa	Canoe
Poppa	Stern
Prua	Bow
Cabina	Cabin

L'aeroplano – Airplane

L'aereo	Airplane
L'elica	Propeller
Le ali	Wings
L'aeroporto	Airport
Il reattore	Reactor
Assistente di volo	Hostess

Taxi

Mi può chiamare un taxi, per favore? - Can you call me a taxi, please?

Quanto costa la corsa fino a? - How much does it cost to take me to?

Mi sembra troppo caro - It looks too expensive

Dove può - Wherever is possible

Per favore mi lasci qui - Drop me here, please

All'angolo - At the corner

Mi fa scendere - Please, let me get down / let me get off

Teach Yourself Italian
UNIT 6

Sento Nostalgia – I am homesick

In this Unit you will learn:

- ❖ To speak in future tense and perfect future, express actions that will take place in the future
- ❖ To use irregular verbs in the future
- ❖ Several useful terms such as adjectives, cardinal and ordinal numbers, math operations and punctuation marks.

Sento Nostalgia

Da pochi giorni sono tornato a Berlino, ma sento già la nostalgia dell'Italia. Non dimenticherò mai tutto quello che hai fatto per me. Dovrò lavorare molto per poter ritornare in Italia, ma certamente ci riuscirò. La prossima volta porterò in vacanza con me la mia sorellina, e sono sicuro che sarà molto contenta di mangiare i deliziosi spaghetti italiani. Ti ringrazio per tutto. Ci rivedremo fra due anni. Un abbraccio. **Daniel.**

Da pochi giorni – a few days ago
Berlino - Berlin
Nostalgia – Nostalgy / Homesick
Ci riuscirò – I will succeed in it
Mia sorellina – My little sister
Sono sicuro – I am sure
Deliziosi - delicious
Ti ringrazio – I thank you
Ci rivedremo – We will see each other
Fra due anni – in two years
Un abbraccio – a hug

Grammar

Simple Future

Simple future for the verbs is formed as follows. The future tense in Italian expresses an action that will take place in the future. Although in English the future is expressed with the helping verb "will" or the phrase "to be going to," in

Teach Yourself Italian

Italian a verb ending marks it as being set in the future tense.

Verbs from the first (-are) and second group (-ere) take the same ending.

Erò

Erai

Erà

Erà

Eremo

Erete

Eranno

Parlerò con te domani - I will speak with you tomorrow

Lui scriverà dopo - He will write later

Verbs from the third group (-ire) take the following ending.

Irò

Irai

Irà

Irà

Iremo

Irete

Iranno

Lei non uscirà stasera - She will not go out tonight or You (polite) will not go out tonight

Loro usciranno stasera- They will go out tonight

Teach Yourself Italian

Irregular verbs in the future

Essere – be	Avere – have	Andare – go	Venire - come
Sarò	Avrò	Andrò	Verrò
Sarai	Avrai	Andrai	Verrai
Sarà	Avrà	Andrà	Verrà
Sarà	Avrà	Andrà	Verrà
Saremo	Avremo	Andremo	Verremo
Sarete	Avrete	Andrete	Verrete
Saranno	Avranno	Andranno	Verranno

Bere - drink	Potere - can	Vedere – see	Sapere - know
Berrò	Potrò	Vedrò	Saprò
Berrai	Potrai	Vedrai	Saprai

Berrà	Potrà	Vedrà	Saprà
Berrà	Potrà	Vedrà	Saprà
Berremo	Potremo	Vedremo	Sapremo
Berrete	Potrete	Vedrete	Saprete
Berranno	Potranno	Vedranno	Sapranno

Pay close attention to these groups of verbs; all similar verbs are conjugated the same way as them into the future.

Verbs that end in ciare (cominciare – start / begin) to make the future.

Io comin**cerò**
Tu comin**cerai**
Lui / lei – Lei comin**cerà**
Noi comin**ceremo**
Voi comin**cerete**
Loro comin**ceranno**

Verbs that end in giare (mangiare - eat) to make the future.

Teach Yourself Italian

Io mangerò
Tu mangerai
Lui / lei – Lei mangerà
Noi mangeremo
Voi mangerete
Loro mangeranno

Verbs that end in care (dimenticare - forget) to make the future.

Io dimenticherò
Tu dimenticherai
Lui / lei – Lei dimenticherà
Noi dimenticheremo
Voi dimenticherete
Loro dimenticheranno

Verbs that end in gare (pagare - pay) to make the future.

Io pagherò
Tu pagherai
Lui / lei – Lei pagherà
Noi pagheremo
Voi pagherete
Loro pagheranno

Simple Perfect

Appena **avrò** terminato, **uscirò** – As soon as finish, I will go out.

Quando **saremo** stati al centro, **passeremo** da casa tua. – When we arrive downtown, we will stop by your house.

Use of the future:
- ✓ Future action: **Domani parlerò con lei di questo** problema – I will talk to her tomorrow about this problem.
- ✓ Imperative – Mandate: **Ora farai tutto ciò che è necessario e perciò non uscirai** – Now, you will do all that it is necessary and that's why you will not go out.
- ✓ Doubt or uncertainty: **Dove sarà ora mia figlia e che cosa farà?** – where would be now my daughter and what would she be doing?

Teach Yourself Italian

Perfect Future

It is formed with the conjugation of the auxiliary verbs **Essere** and **Avere** in the future tense, plus past participle of the verbs.

Essere + Andare	*Avere + Chiedere*
Sarò Andato (a)	Avrò Chiesto
Sarai Andato (a)	Avrai Chiesto
Sarà Andato (a)	Avrà Chiesto
Sarà Andato (a)	Avrà Chiesto
Saremo Andati (e)	Avremo Chiesto
Sarete Andati (e)	Avrete Chiesto
Saranno Andati (e)	Avranno Chiesto

Me ne sarò andato domani alle dieci - By tomorrow at ten, I will be gone.

Loro se ne saranno andate domani a mezzo giorno - By tomorrow at midday, they will be gone.

Lei se ne sarà andata alle nove - She will be gone by nine o'clock.

Remember that when you use the auxiliary **Essere** the past participle must agree in gender and number, while it never changes when used with the auxiliary **Avere**.

Loro avranno parlato con te   They will have spoken with you.

Review Exercises

1. **Complete using the correct form in the future tense.**

   a) Dove abiterai? (a Roma).   ***Abiterò a Roma.***

Teach Yourself Italian

b) A che ora finirete? (alle 7)
   _____

c) Che cosa risponderai? (di no)
   _____

d) Quando verrete? (la settimana prossima) _____

2. Fill in with the correct form in the future tense.

a) Lui--------- (domandare) qualcosa di più.
   Lui domanderà qualcosa di più.

b) Io ti--------- (cercare) domani

c) Tu non------ (dimenticare) mai il mio nome

d) Lei non ti--------- (amare) mai

e) Noi ------- (bere) molta birra

f) Loro------- (vedere) la bellezza

g) Rosanna non----- (comprare) niente

h) Io------- (partire) domani mattina

i) Piero ed io-------- (uscire) di sera

j) Tu------ (salire) in montagna

Vocabulary:

Main prepositions

A - To

Eccetto - Except

Prima di - Before

Nonostante-Malgrado - In spite of

Vicino a - Close to

Con - With

Contro – Against

Di-Da - Of / From

Davanti a - In front of

Fin da - From / since

Dopo - After

Teach Yourself Italian

Dietro il - Behind the

Invece di - Instead of

Sopra il - Over / On

Per - For / By

Tra-Fra - Between

Su-sopra - On

Verso - Toward

Perfino-Persino - Even

Fino a - Until

Dietro - Behind

Per-Da - For / By

Senza - Without

Per mezzo di - By means of

Secondo - According to

I numeri cardinali – Cardinal Numbers

1 Uno	21 Ventuno	108 Centootto
2 Due	22 Ventidue	111 Cento undici
3 Tre	23 Ventitré	200 Duecento
4 Quattro	24 Ventiquattro	300 Trecento
5 Cinque	25 Venticinque	400 Quattrocento
6 Sei	26 Ventisei	500 Cinquecento
7 Sette	27 Ventisette	600 Seicento
8 Otto	28 Ventotto	700 Settecento
9 Nove	29 Ventinove	800 Ottocento
10 Dieci	30 Trenta	900 Novecento
11 Undici	31 Trentuno	1000 Mille
12 Dodici	38 Trentotto	1001 Mille e uno
13 Tredici	40 Quaranta	2000 Duemila
14 Quattordici	50 Cinquanta	3000 Tremila
15 Quindici	60 Sessanta	4000 Quattromila
16 Sedici	70 Settanta	10.000 Diecimila

Teach Yourself Italian

17 Diciassette 80 Ottanta 50.000 Cinquantamila

18 Diciotto 90 Novanta 100.000 Centomila

19 Diciannove 100 Cento 200.000 Duecentomila

20 Venti 101 Centouno 1.000.000 Un milione

1.000.000.000 Un miliardo

2.000.000.000 Due miliardi Ecc...

I numeri Ordinali – *Ordinal Numbers*

1º Primo	14º Quattordicesimo
2º Secondo	20º Ventesimo
3º Terzo	21º Ventunesimo
4º Quarto	22º Ventiduesimo
5º Quinto	30º Trentesimo
6º Sesto	31º Trentunesimo
7º Settimo	40º Quarantesimo

8° Ottavo   50° Cinquantesimo

9° Nono   100° Centesimo

10° Decimo   101° Centunesimo

11° Und**ices**imo   102° Centoduesimo

12° Dodicesimo   300° Trecentesimo

13° Tredicesimo   400° Quattrocentesimo   Ecc...

Le Quattro Operazioni – Math Operations

Quanto fa 5 + (più) 2?   Fa 7   - What is 5 + 2? It is 7.

È un'addizione – **It's an addition**

Quanto fa 9 – (meno) 3?   Fa 6   - What is 9 – 3? It is 6.

È una sottrazione – **It's a subtraction**

Teach Yourself Italian

Quanto fa 3 x (per) 3?   Fa 9   What is 3 x 3? It is 9.

È una moltiplicazione – **It's a multiplication**

Quanto fa 10: (diviso) 2?   Fa 5   What is 10 : 2? It is 5.

È una divisione – **It's a division**

Segni di punteggiatura – Punctuation Marks

,   La virgola   - Comma

;   Il punto e virgola - Semicolon

:   I due punti   - Colon

.	Il punto fermo - Full stop / period
?	Il punto interrogativo - Question mark
!	Il punto esclamativo - Exclamation point
...	I puntini sospensivi - Ellipsis
—	La lineetta - Dash
« »	Le virgolette - Quotation marks
*	L'asterisco - Asterisk
( )	Le parentesi tonde - Parentheses
[ ]	Le parentesi quadre - Brackets
-	Il trattino - Hyphen
´	L'accento acuto - Acute Accent
`	L'accento grave - Grave Accent
'	L'apostrofo - Apostrophe
¨	La dieresi - Diaeresis

Teach Yourself Italian
UNIT 7

La Serata – *A night out*

In this UNIT you will learn:

- ❖ Reflexive verbs
- ❖ Vocabulary for different situations or social events

La Serata

(Dopo essersi riposato un po', Daniel si alza, si lava, si veste e si prepara per uscire).
Sabine: Daniel, come mai ti trovi qui a Berlino? Quanto tempo ti fermi?
Daniel: Mi fermo per tre settimane per lavorare in una fiera. Tu invece di che cosa ti occupi?
Sabine: Io mi occupo di sport, e faccio pugilato.
Daniel: Bellissimo, sono contento per te. Ora, mi piacerebbe organizzare la serata. Ti va di andare a teatro?
Sabine: Non me ne intendo molto di teatro, ma sono sicura che ci divertiremo.

Dopo – after
Qui - here
Quanto tempo – how long
Settimane - weeks
Fiera - fair
Di che cosa ti occupi – what do you do?
Pugilato – boxing
Bellissimo - beautiful
Ora - Now
Teatro – Theater

Grammar

Reflexive Pronouns

Reflexive pronouns are placed before a conjugated verb or attached to the infinitive.

Io **Mi** sveglio   - I wake up (myself)

Tu **Ti** svegli   -   You wake up (yourself)

Lui/Lei **Si** sveglia   - He / She wakes up
(Himself – herself – yourself polite)

Teach Yourself Italian

Noi **Ci** svegliamo   - We wake up (ourselves)

Voi **Vi** svegliate   - You wake up (yourself)

Loro **Si** svegliano   - They wake up (themselves)

Io mi sveglio alle 7   I wake up at seven.

Mi devo svegliare alle 7   (Devo svegliarmi alle 7)   - I must wake up at seven.

Lui mi dà* un libro   He gives me a book.

Dico a voi la verità- Vi dico la verità   Ve la dico (la verità) – I tell you the truth.

* Pay attention to **"dà"** verb and **"da"** preposition.

Simple Past reflexive

Io Mi sono svegliato/svegliata   - I woke up or I have waken up.

Tu Ti sei svegliato/svegliata   - You woke up or You have waken up.

Lui Si è svegliato - He woke up or He has waken up.

Lei Si è svegliata — - She woke up or she has waken up.

Lei Si è svegliato/svegliata — - You woke up or you have waken up (polite).

Noi Ci siamo svegliati/svegliate — - We woke up or We have waken up.

Voi Vi siete svegliati/svegliate — - You woke up or you have waken up (plural).

Loro Si sono svegliati/svegliate — - They woke up or they have waken up.

You always use the auxiliary Essere with this time.

Teach Yourself Italian

Remarks: With Dovere – Potere - Volere in this time, you can use both Essere and Avere.

Mi sono dovuto / dovuta alzare alle 8 – I had to get up at eight.

Ho dovuto alzarmi alle 8 – I had to get up at eight.

Mi sono potuto / potuta alzare alle 8 – I had been able to get up at eight.

Ho potuto alzarmi alle 7 – I had been able to get up at seven.

Mi sono voluto / voluta alzare alle 8 – I had wanted to get up at eight.

Ho voluto alzarmi alle 8 – I had wanted to get up at eight.

Review Exercises

Answer with the correct reflexive pronoun

a) Come ti chiami? (Daniel). ***Mi chiamo Daniel.***

b) Di che cosa ti ricordi? (di tutto)
_____

c) Quanto tempo vi fermate? (due giorni)
_____

d) Di che cosa ti sei occupato? (di medicina) _____

e) Che cosa ti sei messa? (un vestito nuovo) _____

f) Dove vi siete sistemati? (in albergo)
_____

g) A che ora deve alzarsi domani? (alle cinque) _____

h) Mi ami? _____

i) Ci conosci? _____

Teach Yourself Italian

j) Quando chiami la tua amica?

   _____

k) Dove fate gli esercizi?

   _____

Vocabulary:

Cinema

Dov'è il cinema?   - Where is the cinema located?

A che ora iniziano le proiezioni? At what time do the shows start?

L'ultimo spettacolo è alle cinque   - Last show is at five

Si può fumare in sala - Is it allowed to smoke in the room

Teatro - Theater

Voglio andare a teatro - I want to go to the theater

Vorrei prenotare per lo spettacolo - I would like to book the show

Palcoscenico - Stage

Di che secolo è quest'opera ? - From what century is this play?

Museo - Museum

Vietato fumare - It is forbidden to smoke

Che orario fa il museo? - What's the museum timetable?

Quanto dura la mostra? - How long does the exhibition last?

Ci sono guide che parlano l'italiano? - Are there guides who speak Italian?

Teach Yourself Italian

*Qual è la tariffa di una guida? - What is the rate for a tour guide?

Avete un catalogo? - Do you have a catalog?

* Be careful and never write "Qual" with the apostrophe. It does not take it.

UNIT 8

Le Donne hanno la precedenza – Ladies first

In this Unit you will learn how:

- ❖ To use Direct Object Pronouns
- ❖ The Partitive Pronoun or particle ne works
- ❖ To understand the particle plus the pronouns
- ❖ To use There are with the partitive particle ne
- ❖ To learn church vocabulary

Le Donne Hanno La Precedenza

Nicoletta: Pietro, in questo bar vendono i cioccolatini che mi piacciono. Ne compro una scatola. Poi mi accompagni a prendere il taxi?
Pietro: Non hai bisogno di prendere il taxi. Ho la macchina e posso accompagnarti fino all'università.
Salvatore: Ragazzi, quindi mi lasciate solo?
Pietro: Salvatore, mi scuserai se accompagno lei e lascio a piedi te.

Teach Yourself Italian

Salvatore: Certamente, si capisce! Le donne hanno sempre la precedenza!

Cioccolatini – Chocolates
Mi piacciono – I like them
Scatola – Box
Poi – Then
Non hai bisogno – You don't need to
Fino – until
Solo – alone
E lascio a piedi te – and I leave you alone (on foot).

Grammar
Direct Object Pronouns

A direct object is the direct recipient of the action of a verb. A direct object pronoun is placed immediately before a conjugated verb. In a negative sentence, the word **non** must come before the object pronoun.

Mi	
Ti –	
La	conosce bene
Lo	

Pietro	(non)	**La**	aiuta quando può
		Ci	
		Vi	
		Li	
		Le	

Pietro mi aiuta quando può – Peter helps me when he can.

Pietro non ti conosce bene – Peter doesn't know you well.

	Aspetta			*aspetta*	*me.* *te* ***Lei.***
Chi	*Ha salutato*	*Quella signorina?*	*Quel ragazzo*	*ha salutato*	***lui.*** ***lei.*** ***noi.***
	Cerca			*cerca*	***voi.*** ***loro.***

Chi aspetta quella signorina? – Who waits for that young girl?

Quel ragazzo la aspetta. That boy waits for her.

Strong Direct Pronouns

Partitive Pronoun "ne"

Teach Yourself Italian

	Ne		uno
Quanti libri		prendo	alcuni
prendi?			molti
	Non **ne**		nessuno
	Li		Tutti

You use "ne" when you are referring to a portion of a whole, in other words, how many books from a box full of books or from a group of books. Remember, it must agree with gender and number.

Quanti libri prendi? – How many books do you take?

Ne prendo uno – I take one (from the box or group of books, you only take one).

Quante sigarette fumi? – How many cigarettes do you smoke?

Ne fumo molte. – I smoke many (from the package).

The particle CI plus the pronouns MI, TI, VI

Mi accompagni al centro?	Sì, **ti ci** accompagno.
Mi ci accompagni oggi?	Sì, **ti ci** accompagno.

Ci accompagni al centro?	Sì, **vi ci** accompagno.
Ci accompagni al centro oggi?	Sì, **vi ci** accompagno.

Mi ci accompagni oggi? – Do you accompany me there today?

 Sì, **ti ci** accompagno – Yes, I accompany you there.

The particle Ci indicates the place where they are going to (centro).

Mi ci accompagni? Do you accompany me…? Since we know that we are already speaking about Centro, the particle CI indicates the place.

Particle CI plus pronouns LO, LA, LI, LE, NE

		Lo			*Lo*
		La			*La*
		La			*La*
Ci		*Lo*	=	*Ce*	*Lo*
	+	*Le*			*Le*
		Ne			*Ne*

As you can see when using them together, instead of Ci Lo, which is incorrect, we have Ce lo. In other words, the Ci becomes Ce with these

Teach Yourself Italian

pronouns.

Quando accompagni tuo padre al centro? When do you accompany your father downtown?

Ce lo accompagno stasera – *I accompany him this evening (Ce replaces the place and Lo the father).*

Non puoi accompagnarcelo dopo cena? – Can't you accompany him there after dinner?

No, non ce lo posso accompagnare – *No, I cannot accompany him there.*

Ce indicates the place **centro,** and **Lo** indicates the person, **father**.

CI sono – There are with the partitive particle "ne"

			n'è	uno
Quanti	ci sono?	Ce	ne sono	tanti
ragazzi		Non ce	n'è	nessuno
			n'è	una
Quante	ci sono?	Ce	ne sono	tante
ragazze		Non ce	n'è	nessuna

Remember that Ci sono means there are, more than one thing, in other words, plural and Ne is the partitive pronoun, taking something from a whole or a group and it always agrees with gender and number.

Quanti ragazzi ci sono? How many boys are there?
Ce n'è uno - *There is one (from a group, there is only one).*
Quante ragazze ci sono? How many girls are there?
Non ce n'è nessuna - *There are none (from a group)*

Vocabulary:

Chiesa - Church

Potrebbe indicarmi una chiesa? - Could you show me a church?

Qual è l'orario del culto? - What is the time for the service?

È vietato bere in chiesa - It is forbidden to drink in the church

È possibile visitare la chiesa? - Is it possible to visit the church?

Dio – God

Gesù - Jesus

Teach Yourself Italian

Spirito Santo – Holy Spirit

Religione – Religion

Angelo - Angel

Bibbia - Bible

Diavolo - Devil

Inferno – Hell

Vangelo - Gospel

Benedizione – Blessing

Funerale- Funeral

Messa – Mass

Nozze – Wedding

Predica - Sermon

Vespro – Eve

                    Cielo - Heaven

UNIT 9

Non La Sopporto – I can't stand her

In this Unit you will learn how:

- ❖ To use Direct pronouns in past tense, past participle, Simple Past or Present Perfect Simple.
- ❖ General vocabulary on Hotel, Restaurants and Menu.

Non La Sopporto

Pietro: Chiara, ti ho detto tante volte che Luigi mi è antipatico. Ci siamo incontrati spesso per strada e non mi ha mai guardato.
Chiara: Pazienza! Tu non sopporti lui, e io non sopporto la sua fidanzata Jessica. Se ci mettiamo a discutere, faremo tardi e non potremo entrare allo spettacolo. Hai comprato i biglietti per stasera, giusto?
Pietro: Sì, certo che li ho comprati. Ma dove li ho messi?
Chiara: Eccoli qui mio caro.

Per strada – on the street

Teach Yourself Italian

Pazienza - patience
Fidanzata – girlfriend - fiancée
Discutere – argue
I biglietti – tickets
Stasera - tonight
Giusto – right, correct
Eccoli qui mio caro – here they are, my darling

Grammar

Direct pronouns in past tense.

LO, LA, LI, LE plus the verb in past participle.
Hai comprato **il libro**? – Have you bought the book or did you buy the book?
Sì, **l'**ho comprat**o**. – Yes, I have bought it or Yes, I bought it.
Oggi alle cinque, avrai finito **gli esercizi**? By five o'clock today, will you have finished the exercises or by five o'clock today, will you have completed the exercises?
Sì, **li** avrò finit**i**. – Yes, I would have finished them or Yes, I will have finished them.
Avete ricevuto **la comunicazione**? – Have you

received the communication or did you receive the communication?

Sì, l'abbiamo ricevuta. – Yes, we have received it or Yes, we received it.

Avete ospitato **le vostre cugine**? - Have you hosted your cousins or did you host your cousins?

No, non **le** abbiamo ospitate. – No, we have not hosted them or No, we did not host them.

Remark: it is very important to pay close attention to gender and number, everything must match.

MI, TI, CI, VI, LA plus the verb in Simple Past or Present Perfect Simple

Perché non mi hai salutato/a? – why have you not greeted me or why did you not greet me?
 Scusa, ma non t'avevo riconosciuto (a) – Excuse me, but I have not recognized you or Excuse me, but I did not recognize you.
Perché non ci hai salutato/e? - Why have you not greeted us or why did you not greet us?
Scusa, ma non vi avevo visto (e) – Excuse me, but I have not seen you or Excuse me, but I did not see you (plural).

Teach Yourself Italian

Remark: it is very important to pay close attention to gender and number, everything must match.

Partitive pronoun "ne" plus the verb in Simple Past or Present Perfect Simple

Quanti fogli hai comprato? – How many sheets have you bought or how many sheets did you buy?

Non **ne** ho comprato nessuno. – I have not bought any or I did not buy any (from a group).

Quante sigarette hai comprato? – How many cigarettes have you bought or how many cigarettes did you buy?

Ne ho comprate molte. – I have bought many or I bought many (from a package).

Remark: it is very important to pay close attention to gender and number, everything must match.

Vocabulary

Albergo - Hotel

Dove posso trovare un buon albergo? - Where can I find a good hotel?

Desidero una camera singola - I would like a single room

Matrimoniale - Double room

Con bagno e doccia - With bath and shower

Quanto costa per una notte? - How much does it cost per night?

È inclusa nel prezzo la colazione? - Is breakfast included in the price?

Vorrei una camera con vista sul mare - I would like an ocean view room

Va bene, prenderò questa - It is ok, I will reserve this one

Desidero essere svegliato alle nove - I would like a wake up call at 9:00

Teach Yourself Italian

Vorrei un asciugamano — I would like a towel

La chiave, per favore — The key, please

Ci sono messaggi per me? — Are there any messages for me?

Il conto, per favore — The bill, please

Ristorante - Restaurant

Un buon ristorante — A good restaurant

Avete un tavolo libero per due? — Do you have a table for two?

Abbiamo molta fretta — We are really in a hurry

Mi porta il menù e la lista dei vini? — Can you bring me the menu and the wine list, please?

Potrei avere un tovagliolo? — Could I have a napkin?

Un piatto — A plate

Una forchetta — A fork

Un cucchiaio - A spoon

Un coltello - A knife

L'olio - Oil

L'aceto - Vinegar

Il sale - Salt

Il pepe - Pepper

Uno stuzzicadenti - Toothpick

Vorrei l'acqua minerale - I would like mineral water

Una birra piccola - A small beer

Avete qualche specialità della casa? - Do you have any house special?

Com'è fatta, cosa contiene? - How is it done, what are the ingredients?

Cameriere mi porta il conto, per favore? - Waiter, can you bring me the bill, please?

Teach Yourself Italian

C'è un errore nel conto   -   There's a mistake in the bill

Non lascia niente di mancia?   - Don't you leave a tip?

Il resto è per te   - The change is for you.

Menù - Menu

Acqua	Water	Aragosta	Lobster
Arancia	Orange	Banana	Banana
Birra	Beer	Biscotti	Cookies
Bistecca	Steak	Bottiglia	Bottle
Brodo	Broth	Burro	Butter
Caramelle	Candies	Cavolfiore	Cauliflower
Cena	Dinner	Cipolla	Onion
Costoletta	Cutlet - chop	Pasticcini	Pastries

Patate fritte   French fries   Pepe   Pepper

Zuppa di pesce - Fish Soup   Vino rosso - Red wine

Trota   Trout   Uovo   Egg

Riso   Rice   Pollo arrosto   Roast chicken

Fagioli   Beans   Cuoco   Cook

Fegato   Liver   Formaggio   Cheese

Funghi – Mushrooms   Fragole - Strawberries

Frittata   Omelette   Gelato   Ice cream

Gamberetti – Shrimps

Insalata russa   Russian salad

Granoturco   Corn   Maiale   Pork

Mela   Apple

Melanzana   Aubergine / Eggplant

Olive   Olives   Ostriche   Oysters

Teach Yourself Italian

Peperoni	Peppers	Avocado - Avocado
Torta	Pie / Cake	Tacchino	Turkey
Pomodori	Tomatoes	Pranzo	Lunch
Piselli	Peas	Gallina	Hen

UNIT 10

Voglia di Uscire – Wish to go out

In this UNIT you will learn:

- ❖ Imperfect, past perfect and conditional tense of verbs.
- ❖ Different vocabulary to increase your learning process.

Voglia di Uscire

Pietro: Sei uscita ieri sera?
Nicoletta: No, Pietro, non sono uscita, perché non ne avevo voglia.
Pietro: Hai voglia di uscire oggi? Andiamo al cinema?
Nicoletta: Certamente, vado pazza per i film gialli. Ho visto un film dove l'assassino uccideva le donne, ma prima le strozzava...
Pietro: Come le strozzava? Qual era il titolo, e come si chiamava il regista?

Teach Yourself Italian

Nicoletta: Non ricordo, perché il film era già cominciato. Poi mi sono addormentata, e quando mi sono svegliata il film era già finito...

Ieri sera – *Yesterday evening*
Avevo voglia – *I wanted*
Oggi - *Today*
Vado pazza per – *I am crazy for*
I film gialli – *Crime films / Thrillers*
L'assassino – *The killer* – *assassin*
Uccideva – *Killed (them)*
Donne - *women*
Strozzava – *Strangled them*
Qual era il titolo? – *What was the title?*
Il regista – *The director*
Già – *Already*

Grammar

Imperfect Time - Past

This time is formed by using the following combinations for each group of verbs (as shown below):

First Group	Second Group	Third Group
ARE	**ERE**	**IRE**
Avo	Evo	Ivo
Avi	Evi	Ivi
Ava	Eva	Iva
Ava	Eva	Iva
Avamo	Evamo	Ivamo
Avate	Evate	Ivate
Avano	Evano	Ivano

Io parlavo con te - I spoke with you or I used to speak with you.

Teach Yourself Italian

Tu credevi a loro   - You believed in them or you used to believe in them.

Lui partiva ogni sabato   - He left every Saturday or He used to leave every Saturday.

Lei pensava a me - She thought about me or She used to think about me.

Even when this time is represented as a simple past in English, do not get confused and practice it very well, because in Italian it represents more a past continuous action.

Verbs Essere and Avere in the imperfect time

Essere	**Avere**
Ero	Avevo
Eri	Avevi

Era	Aveva
Era	Aveva
Eravamo	Avevamo
Eravate	Avevate
Erano	Avevano

Past Perfect

Quando la luce è tornata, il film era già finito da un pezzo - When the light came back, the film was already long gone
Ieri ero stanco perché avevo lavorato troppo. – I was tired yesterday, because I had worked too much.

Preterit Perfect

It is formed with the Past Perfect of the verbs **Essere** and **Avere,** plus the past participle of the verb.

Teach Yourself Italian

Essere + Andare *Avere + Parlare*

Ero   Andato (a)   Avevo   Parlato

Eri   Andato (a)   Avevi   Parlato

Era   Andato (a)   Aveva   Parlato

Era   Andato (a)   Aveva   Parlato

Eravamo Andati (e)   Avevamo   Parlato

Eravate Andati (e)   Avevate   Parlato

Erano Andati (e)   Avevano   Parlato

Avevo parlato con te - I had talked to you

Ero già partito alle sei - I had been gone at six

Review Exercise

Complete using the correct form of the verb in the imperfect tense.

   a) Che cosa facevi quando ti ho telefonato? (preparare il pranzo)
   Preparavo il pranzo.

   b) Con chi parlavi quando ti ho visto al cinema? (parlare con gli amici)

c) Che cosa facevi mentre io studiavo? (ascoltare musica)

d) Dove mangiavi quando eri in centro? (al ristorante)

e) Chi ti curava quando stavi male? (il dottore)

Vocabulary:

Banca - Bank

Potrebbe indicarmi una banca? - Could you show me a bank?

A che sportello devo andare? - What window /counter should I go to?

Vorrei cambiare denaro - I would like to change money

Vorrei prelevare dalla mia carta di credito - I would like to withdraw from my credit card

Teach Yourself Italian

Mi può dare soldi spicci? - Can you give me coins?

Posso aprire un conto? - Can I open an account?

Feste - Holidays

Capodanno	New Year's Day
Carnevale	Carnival
Compleanno	Happy Birthday
Natale	Christmas
Pasqua	Easter
Pentecoste	Pentecost
Vacanze	Holidays
Vigilia	Christmas Eve
Tanti auguri	Congratulations / Best wishes / Many happy returns

Corrispondenza - Correspondence

Caro Signore	Dear Sir – Mr.
Egregio Signore	Dear Sir
Gentile Signorina	Dear Miss

Sincere congratulazioni - Candid Congratulations

Vivissimi auguri   - Heartfelt Wishes

Cordiali saluti   - Best Regards

Cari saluti   - Best Wishes

Affari - Business

Potrei parlare con l'amministratore?   Could I speak with the manager?

Sono il rappresentante della ditta - I am the representative of the company

Teach Yourself Italian

Deve fissare un appuntamento - You have to make an appointment

Sono lieto di conoscerla - I am pleased to meet you

Mi può preparare un preventivo? - Can you prepare me a quote?

Non c'è nulla di meno caro? - Is there something cheaper?

Mi può fare uno sconto? - Can you give me a discount?

Condizioni di pagamento - Payment terms

Posso dare un anticipo? - Can I make an upfront payment?

Quando è pronta la merce? - When will the merchandise be ready?

Qual è l'orario dei negozi? - What's the business working hours?

Dov'è il supermercato più vicino? - Where is the closest supermarket?

La mia taglia è - My size is

Posso provarlo? - Can I try it on?

C'è lo sconto - There's a discount

Può farmi un pacchetto regalo? - Can you wrap it up in a gift package?

Posso pagare con la carta di credito? - Can I pay with the credit card?

Vorrei un paio di scarpe da uomo - I would like a pair of men's shoes

Sono troppo lunghi - They are too long

Lunghi - Long

Teach Yourself Italian

Corte - Short

Ecco questo paio mi va bene - Ok, this pair fits me

Vorrei un cappello da uomo - I would like a man's hat

Vorrei un quaderno a righe - I would like a ruled-exercise book

Avete un portacenere? - Do you have an ashtray?

Vorrei una borsetta - I would like a small handbag

Cintura - Belt

Quando è pronto - When is it ready?

Vorrei tagliare i capelli - I would like to get a haircut

Barba - Beard

Non troppo corta - Not too short

Fate trattamenti di manicure/pedicure? Do you do manicure/pedicure?

Avete una cipria? - Do you have face powder?

Telefono-Posta – Telephone - Post

Dov'è l'ufficio postale? - Where is the post office?

C'è una cassetta delle lettere? - Is there a mailbox?

Desidero francobolli per l'estero - I would like stamps for abroad

Vorrei spedire questo pacco - I would like to ship this package

Teach Yourself Italian

Dov'è un telefono? - Where is the nearest telephone?

Vorrei telefonare in Italia - I would like to call Italy

Potrebbe riprovare? - Could you redial?

Mi chiama questo numero? - Can you call this number?

Vorrei inviare un fax - I would like to send a fax

Pronto, chi parla? - Hello, who's speaking?

Sono...e vorrei parlare con... - I am… and I would like to speak with…

Non si sente bene - I can't hear you well

Potrebbe parlare più forte? - Could you speak louder?

Richiami appena può - Call back as soon as you can, please

Ti telefonerò più tardi - I will call you back later

Aspettavo una telefonata da te - I was expecting a call from you

No, ora non è in casa - No, he (she) is not home at the moment

L'ho sempre trovato occupato - I have always found it busy

Posso richiamare più tardi? - Can I call back later?

Teach Yourself Italian
UNIT 11

Cosa Vorresti Fare? – What would you like to do?

In this Unit you will learn how:

- ❖ To use the Present Conditional and Present Perfect Conditional
- ❖ The correct use of the conditional tense
- ❖ General vocabulary to increase your learning skills

Cosa vorresti fare?

Daniel: Che programmi hai per il futuro?
Pietro: Vorrei diventare uno scienziato.
Daniel: Ti piacerebbe lavorare anche all'estero?
Pietro: Sì, molto. E tu cosa vorresti fare?
Daniel: Mi piacerebbe diventare uno specialista in meccanica, anche perché mio padre avrebbe voluto vedermi all'università, e per questo motivo vorrei laurearmi al più presto.

Che – what
Programmi - plans
Diventare - become

> Uno scienziato – a scientist
> Ti piacerebbe – would you like
> All'estero - abroad
> Uno specialista in meccanica – a mechanic specialist
> Per questo motivo – for this reason
> Laurearmi - graduate
> Al più presto – as soon as possible

Grammar

Present Conditional

This time corresponds to the English Would and it is formed as follows:

For the First Group -**Are** drop the final -e in its infinitive form and change the a- into an e-. For the Second Group -**Ere** just drop the final -e in its infinitive form, then add the appropriate ending.

Erei

Eresti

Teach Yourself Italian

Erebbe

Erebbe

Eremmo

Ereste

Erebbero

Parlerei con te - I would speak with you

Vorrei parlare con te - I would like to speak with you

Vorresti una birra? - Would you like a beer?

Crederei alle tue parole - I would believe in your words – I'd believe in your words.

For the Third Group -**Ire** drop the final -e in its infinitive form, and add the appropriate ending.

Irei

Iresti

Irebbe

Irebbe

Iremmo

Ireste

Irebbero

Partiresti con me?   - Would you leave with me?

Present Perfect Conditional
This time indicates situations and events regarded only as potential and subject to a condition. Besides indicating events no longer possible, it is used to indicate the future in the past.

Teach Yourself Italian

Ieri avrei studiato volentieri, ma mi sono dimenticato (a). – I would have studied willingly yesterday, but I forgot.

Ieri sarei partito (a), ma c'era lo sciopero dei bus e pioveva. – I would have left yesterday, but there was a bus strike and it was raining.

Use of the conditional:

- ✓ Wish: Vorrei imparare l'italiano – I would like to learn Italian.
- ✓ Request: Salve signorine, potrei farvi qualche domanda? – Hello Misses, could I ask you some questions?
- ✓ Doubts: Oggi potrei venire *da te, ma non sono sicura – I could come to you today, but I am not sure.
- ✓ Personal Opinion: Direi che lei è più bella – I would say that she's more beautiful.

  *Rember: Da te means at your house.

Volerci – To be necessary

	Vuole	Un'ora per finire il
	Vorrà	lavoro – **An hour to**
	Vorrebbe	**finish the work** *is*
Ci		*needed.*

		Molto denaro per studiare medicina – **A lot of money to study medicine *is needed.***
Sarebbe È	Voluto	Molto denaro per studiare medicina
	Voluta	Un'ora per risolvere il problema – **An hour to solve the problem wa*s needed.***
Vogliono Vorranno Vorrebbero		Tre ore per risolvere questo problema
		Molti soldi per studiare medicina
Sarebbero Sono	Volute	Tre ore per risolvere questo problema
	Voluti	Molti soldi per fare il giro del mondo – **A lot of money to travel around the**

Teach Yourself Italian
world *was needed.*

Review Exercise

Complete using the conditional tense

a) Perché non studi? (sono stanco) – Studierei, ma sono stanco.

b) Perché non aspetti? (ho fretta)

c) Perché non leggete? (abbiamo sonno)

d) Perché non uscite? (volere riposare)

e) Perché non partite? (non stiamo bene)

f) Noi usciamo. Voi uscireste con noi?

g) Noi aspettiamo. Voi aspettereste con noi?

h) Quando potresti venire? (stasera)

i) Perché non sei uscita? (dovere studiare)

j) Perché non ti sei fermata ancora? (dovevo andare via)

Vocabulary

Caffetteria - Cafeteria   *- Bar – Bar*

Birreria – Beer Center

Un po' di zucchero	- A little sugar
Quanto costa l'entrata?	- How much is the entrance?
Avete panini imbottiti?	- Do you have sandwiches?
Il signore desidera?	- What would you like Sir?
Cosa prende?	- What would you take?
Lei fuma?	- Do you smoke?
Posso offrirle una sigaretta?	- Can I offer you a cigarrette?

Teach Yourself Italian

Grazie, ma non fumo smoke.	- Thanks, but I don't
Posso invitarla a ballare?	- Can I ask you to dance?
Signorina, è sola?	- Miss, Are you alone?
Gli piace ballare?	- Do you like to dance?
Che cosa posso offrirle?	- What can I offer you?
Io non so ballare dance.	- I don't know how to
Vuole uscire con me?	- Would you like to go out with me?
È fidanzata?	- Do you have a boyfriend?
È sposata?	- Are you married?
Ha figli?	- Do you have children?

Come si chiamano? - What are their names?

Parla l'inglese? - Do you speak English?

Mi piacerebbe vederla ancora - I would like to see you again

La posso accompagnare a casa? - Can I take you home?

Posso telefonarle? - Can I call you?

Che numero ha? - What's your number?

Posso invitarla a pranzo? - Can I invite you for lunch?

Se mi dà l'email, le scrivo - If you give me your emai, I will write you-

Le manderò una cartolina - I will send you a postcard

Spero di ritornare presto - I hope to be back soon

Teach Yourself Italian

Cameriere, ha un fiammifero? - Waiter, do you have matches?

Visite - Visits

Vuole venire oggi a casa mia? - Do you want to come to my place today?

Vuole venire oggi da me*? - Do you want to come to my house today?

A prendere una tazza di té - To take the tea

Un cocktail - A cocktail

A cena - A dinner

Grazie, molto volentieri - Thanks, willingly.

Mi dispiace, ma ho già un impegno - I am sorry, but I already busy

Posso venire domani? - Can I come tomorrow?

Buongiorno	- Good morning
Buon pomeriggio	- Good Afternoon
Prego, si accomodi	- Go ahead, take a seat

È stata una piacevole serata - It has been a lovely evening.

* Remember that in Italian we use this kind of expression "da me, dai miei nonni, dai miei amici" to say that we are at somebody's house.

Teach Yourself Italian

UNIT 12

Macchina in Prestito – A borrowed car

In this UNIT you will learn:

- ❖ To recognize familiy members
- ❖ Indirect and articulated pronouns
- ❖ Different vocabulary

Macchina in prestito

Daniel: Mi faresti un favore?
Pietro: Volentieri!
Daniel: Mi presteresti la tua macchina? La mia è rotta.
Pietro: Certo che te la presto. Ma fai attenzione, sii prudente!
Daniel: Non ti preoccupare, te la riporterò tutta intera.
Pietro: Lo spero, mi fido di te, altrimenti non te la farei usare.
Daniel: Grazie tante, grazie mille.

Un favore – a favour
La tua macchina – your car
La mia è rotta – mine is broken
Ma fai attenzione – but pay attention
Sii prudente – be careful
Non ti preoccupare – don't worry
Te la riporterò tutta intera – I'll bring it back in one piece.
Lo spero – I hope so
Mi fido di te – I trust you
Altrimenti – if not / on the contrary
Non te la farei usare – I would not allow you to use it.
Grazie tante, grazie mille – Thanks a lot.

Grammar

Indirect Object Pronouns

Indirect Object Nouns and Pronouns answer the question to whom? Or for whom? In English, the word "to" is sometimes omitted.

Mi	invia un pacco – **sends me a package**
Ti	presta la macchina – **lends**

Marco		**Teach Yourself Italian** you the car
	Gli	regala un accendino – **gives him a lighter**
	Le	mostra quello che ha fatto – **shows her what he's done.**
	Ci	dice di sì – **tells us yes**
	Vi	risponde sempre di no – **always answers you no.**
	Gli*	augura la buona notte – **wishes them a good night.**

* In current Italian usage, the use of *gli* in place of *loro* is normal. In spoken and casual language *gli* also tends to substitute the singular feminine form *le*. However, in written and formal Italian it's best to maintain the distinction between *gli* - *le*. Also because it is important to maintain the difference between feminine and masculine forms.

| pensi? | Penso | **a me** |

A chi	hai detto quelle parole?	Le ho dette	**a te / a Lei**
	piacciono le fragole?	Piacciono	**a lui** **a lei** **a noi** **a voi** **a loro**

A chi pensi? - **Whom do you think of?**
Penso a te – **I think of you.**

When the Indirect Pronouns Mi – Ti – Si – Ci – Vi - Gli are used with the articles Lo – La – Li – Le – Ne, then change. See the chart with the changes below.

Me lo	Te lo	Se lo	Ce lo	Ve lo	Glielo
Me la	Te la	Se la	Ce la	Ve la	Gliela
Me li	Te li	Se li	Ce li	Ve li	Glieli
Me le	Te le	Se le	Ce le	Ve le	Gliele
Me ne	Te ne	Se ne	Ce ne	Ve ne	Gliene

Teach Yourself Italian

Marco gli regala un libro – **Marco gives them a book.**

Glielo compra domani – **He will buy it for them tomorrow.**

Review Exercises

Complete using the correct form of the Indirect Pronoun

a) Quando parlerai alla segretaria? (fra poco) – **Le parlerò fra poco.**

b) Che cosa darai a Daniela? (una rosa)

c) Quando risponderai al tuo amico? (domani)

d) Mi presti la tua macchina o la moto? (la macchina)

e) Mi dici la verità o una bugia? (la verità)

f) Che cosa ci offrirete? (un gelato)

g) Che cosa mi manderà? (un regalo)

h) Vi piacciono questi fiori? (sì)

i) Le è piaciuto il viaggio? (sì, mi)

j) Vi sono piaciuti quei vini? (no, non ci)

k) Che cosa hai regalato alla fidanzata? (un bracciale)

l) Che cosa mi ha spedito? (una cartolina)

m) Professore, per favore, vorrei parlar_____.

n) Marco guardava la ragazza e _____ sorrideva.

o) È maleducato: quando _____ parlo, lui non _____ risponde mai.

p) Devi imparare a non toccare le cose che non _____ appartengono.

Vocabulary

Teach Yourself Italian
Famiglia - Family

Antenati - Ancestors

Bisnonno (a) - Great grandfather/grandmother

Cognato (a) - Brother/Sister in law

Cugino (a) - Cousin

Fidanzato (a) - Boyfriend/Girlfriend

Figlio (a) - Son/Daughter

Fratello - Brother

Sorella - Sister

Genitori - Parents

Madre - Mother

Mamma - Mom

Matrigna - Stepmother

Patrigno - Stepfather

Marito - Husband

Zio (a) - Uncle/Aunt

Moglie - Wife

Nipote di zio (a) - Uncle's Nephew/Niece

Nipotino (a) - Nephew/Niece

Nonno (a) - Grandfather/Grandmother

Nubile - Single

Nuora - Daughter in law

Padre - Father

Papà - Dad

Parente - Relative

Scapolo - Bachelor

Sposo (a) - Husband/Wife

Suocero (a) - Stepfather

Teach Yourself Italian

* The nouns with (a) in brackets mean that you just need to change O by A and you will have the feminine version of that noun.

UNIT 13

Un Ladro – A Thief

In this UNIT you will learn:

- ❖ Prepositional Articles
- ❖ Different vocabulary to improve your learning skills

Un Ladro

(Piero, ladro ben noto alla polizia, si trova di nuovo al commissariato).
Piero: Va bene commissario, Le dirò tutto. Domenica a mezzogiorno sono entrato in casa della mia vicina per rubarle i gioielli. Ma, non mi caverà una parola di bocca sui miei complici...
Commissario: Ti conviene parlare. Raccontami per filo e per segno quello che è successo.
Piero: Mi scusi commissario, ma non posso dirle altro.
Commissario: Non fare storie! Come hai trovato le chiavi?
Piero: Me le ha date... non posso parlare...
Commissario: Chi te le ha date?

Teach Yourself Italian

Piero: Il mio collega di lavoro, il marito della vicina!

Commissario: Il marito? Impossibile! Perché avrebbe dovuto farlo?

Ladro – thief
Ben noto – well known
Polizia - Police
Di nuovo - again
Al commissariato – At police station
Commissario – Chief of police
Mia vicina – my neighbour
Per rubarle – to steal from her
I gioielli – the jewels
Non mi caverà una parola di bocca – I will not say a word
Complici - accomplices
Per filo e per segno – in great details (backwards and forwards)
Dirle altro – tell you more
Collega di lavoro – co-worker
Impossibile - impossible

Grammar

Prepositional Articles :

Quanti libri?		**Me**	l'		mandati molti
Quante lettere?	Pietro (non)	te **glie** ve	l' li le	ha	spedite molte
Il libro?		ve	ne		mandato a scuola
La lettera?					spedita nessuna.

Always remember that everything must match gender and number.

Il libro? - The book?

Pietro me l'ha mandato a scuola – Pietro sent it to me at the school.

Quanti libri? – How many books?

Pietro me ne ha mandati molti – Pietro sent to me many of them.

* Molti – many (masculine plural)
* Molte – many (feminine plural)

Vocabulary

Teach Yourself Italian
Persone di Servizio – Service Staff

Autista - Driver

Bambinaia - Babysitter

Domestico   - Servant

Facchino - Bellman

Giardiniere   - Gardener

Portiere   Porter

Affitto   - Rent

Bagno   - Bathroom

Camera da letto   -Bedroom

Cantina   - Cellar

Corridoio   -Corridor

Cortile   -Courtyard

Cucina   -Kitchen

Finestra   -Window

Mobili	-Furniture
Parete	-Wall
Piano	-Floor
Pianterreno	-Ground floor
Porta	-Door
Sala	-Room
Sala da pranzo	-Dining room
Soggiorno	-Living room
Scala	-Staircase
Stanza	-Room
Letto	-Bed
Toilette	-Rest room
Trasloco	-Moving
Cassetto	-Drawer

Teach Yourself Italian

Chiave	-Key
Serratura	-Lock

Oggetti - Objects

Presa di corrente	Outlet
Voltaggio	Voltage
Cucina a gas	Gas Kitchen
Fornello	Stove
Ferro da stiro	Iron
Frigorifero	Refrigerator
Lampada	Lamp
Lampadario	Chandelier
Lampadina	Light bulb
Lavatrice	Washing Machine
Pavimento	Floor
Pentola	Pot
Poltrona	Armchair
Scaldabagno	Water Heater
Tappeto	Carpet

Tavolo	Table
Vetro	Glass
Divano	Sofa

Teach Yourself Italian
UNIT 14

Non Mi Faccia Male – *Don't hurt me*

In this UNIT you will learn:

- ❖ To give orders using the imperative of verbs
- ❖ Different vocabulary, signs and warnings.

Non Mi Faccia Male

Segretaria: Intanto si accomodino in questa saletta e abbiate un po' di pazienza.
Paziente: Mi raccomando, dottore, non mi faccia male.
Dottore: Non si preoccupi. Mi faccia vedere. Vada nella stanza accanto e così la visito. Ritengo necessario fare una radiografia. Mercedes, venga qui per favore!
Segretaria: Dica, dottore!
Dottore: C'è bisogno di una radiografia per questa signorina; la accompagni dal radiologo e poi mi porti immediatamente la lastra, grazie.
Segretaria: Signorina, venga con me. Stia tranquilla e non si preoccupi. La porto a fare la

radiografia e poi parlerà del risultato con il dottore, quando avrà finito.

Intanto - Meanwhile
Saletta – small room
Un po' – a little
Mi raccomando – I beg you
Dottore - doctor
Non mi faccia male – don't hurt me
Non si preoccupi – don't worry
Mi faccia vedere – let me see
Stanza - room
Accanto – next
Radiografia – X-ray
Dica, dottore – speak, doctor
Radiologo - Radiologist
La lastra – The plate
Stia tranquilla – Be still / Keep Calm
Risultato – result

Grammar

Teach Yourself Italian
Imperative with Lei and Loro.

The imperative is used to give orders, advice and exhortation.

Parlare	Scrivere	Partire	Finire
Lui/Lei Parl*i*	Scriv*a*	Part*a*	Finisc*a*
Loro Parl*ino*	Scriv*ano*	Part*ano*	Finisc*ano*

For verbs from the -Are group, just remove the infinitive Are and add the ending I or Ino.

Parli Italiano – **Speak Italian** (a command to you polite)

Parlino Inglese – **Speak English** (a command to them)

For verbs from the -Ere and -Ire groups, just remove the infinitive Ere or Ire and add the ending A o Ano.

Scriva la lettera – **write the letter** (a command to you polite)

Scrivano l'email – **write the email** (a command to them)

Parta oggi – **leave today** (a command to you polite)

Partano domani – **leave tomorrow** (a command to them)

Pay special attention to the verbs in the third group (-Ire) that take the suffix Isc.

Finisca di mangiare – **Finish eating** (a command to you polite)

Finiscano di parlare – **Finish speaking** (a command to them)

Remember to use the imperative when giving a:

- ✓ Command or invitation: **Si accomodi qui e attenda** – make yourself comfortable and wait.

- ✓ Advice: **Mi ascolti, aspetti un momento prima di partire** – Listen to me, wait a moment before leaving.

- ✓ Pleading: **Mi raccomando dottore, non mi faccia male** – I beg you doctor, don't hurt me.

Imperative and Pronouns

Teach Yourself Italian

Se è stanco, **si accomodi** e **riposi** – if you are tired, make yourself comfortable and rest.

Fumatevi una sigaretta, ma **fumatela** fuori! – Smoke a cigarette, but smoke it outside.

Review Exercise

Complete with the correct form of the imperative

a) Potrei pagare oggi? Va bene, _____**paghi**_____ pure.

b) Potremmo aspettare ancora? Va bene, _____ pure.

c) Possiamo mangiare questi pasticcini? E perché no, _____ pure.

d) Posso fumare una sigaretta? E perché no, _____ pure.

e) Se vuoi studiare, _____.

f) Se vuoi telefonare, _____.

g) Se hai voglia di leggere,
   _____.

h) Se hai voglia di dormire,
   _____.

i) Se dobbiamo entrare,
   _____.

j) Se dobbiamo smettere,
   _____.

k) Se volete correre,
   _____.

l) Se non volete tornare,
   _____.

m) Se dobbiamo fermarci,
   _____.

n) Se non vuoi invitare Daniel,
   _____.

o) Se vuoi andare a casa,
   _____.

p) Se vuoi fare questo lavoro,
   _____subito.

q) Se vuoi dire la verità, _____
   subito.

Teach Yourself Italian

Vocabulary:

Circolazione - Circulation

Dov'è la piazza? - Where is the square?

Il supermercato - The supermarket

È lontano o vicino? -   Is it far or near?

Mi scusi, mi sono perso - Excuse me, I got lost.

Può dirmi dove sono? - Can you tell me where I am?

Devo girare a destra o sinistra - Should I turn right or left?

Casa - House

Avete appartamenti in affitto? - Do you have apartments for rent?

Ammobiliato o vuoto? - Furnished or empty?

Posso vedere l'appartamento? - Can I see the apartment?

A che piano è? - In what floor is it?

L'affitto si paga in anticipo - The rent is paid in advance

Bisogna versare una cauzione - You need to make an upfront deposit

Quando potrò occupare l'appartamento? When can I move in to the apartment?

Ha il telefono? - Does it come with the telephone service?

È compreso nel prezzo? - Is it included in the price?

C'è un portinaio - There's a porter

Il portone — Front Gate / Door

La scala — Staircase

Il soggiorno — Living room

Camera da letto — Bedroom

Teach Yourself Italian

Il gabinetto	Toilet/Restroom
La cucina	Kitchen
Il balcone	Balcony
Il bagno	Bathroom
Il corridoio	Corridor
La finestra	Window
Il tetto	Roof
L'ascensore	Elevator
La porta	Door
La sala d'ingresso	Entrance room
La stanza	Room
L'appartamento	Apartment
La dispensa	Pantry
Il camino	Chimney

La cantina	Cellar
Il cortile	Courtyard
Il piano	Floor
L'ultimo piano	Top floor
L'attico	Top floor
La sala da pranzo	Dining room
La parete	Wall
La facciata	The front / façade
Il muro	Wall
La Presa	Socket
Il cornicione	Cornice

La scuola - School

Teach Yourself Italian

L'edificio scolastico	School Building
L'aula	Classroom
Il banco	Desk
La lavagna	Blackboard
Il gesso	Chalk
La carta geografica	Map
Il mappamondo	World map
L'alunno	Student
Il professore	Teacher
Il preside	Dean
Il direttore	Principal
La scolaresca	Pupils
La scuola elementare	Elementary school
La scuola media	Secondary school
L'istituto tecnico	Technical Institute

L'istituto magistrale - Teacher training Institute

Il liceo artistico - Artistic Highschool

L'accademia delle Belle Arti   Art School

Il conservatorio di musica Music Conservatory

L'università   University

La facoltà di lettere - Faculty of Literature

Facoltà di giurisprudenza o diritto   Faculty of law

Di filosofia   - Philosophy

Di Medicina   - Medicine

Di ingegneria   - Engineering

La matita   - Pencil

Penna stilografica - Fountain Pen / Ink Pen

Il quaderno   - Copybook

Il quaderno di appunti   - Notebook

Teach Yourself Italian

La lezione — - Lesson

La spiegazione del professore — Teacher's explanation

La prova d'esame — - Exam

Gli esami di laurea — - To present one's thesis", "academic exams".

UNIT 15

Sulla Spiaggia – On the Beach

In this UNIT you will learn:

- ❖ To use the imperative plus irregular verbs in this time.
- ❖ New vocabulary

Sulla Spiaggia

Pietro: Passami quella valigia e prendi la radio. Andiamo sulla spiaggia!
Sabine: E dove la metto?
Pietro: Dalla a me, non ti preoccupare. La poso nel portabagagli!
Sabina: Va bene, grazie Pietro! Allora metti un po' di musica e partiamo!
Pietro: Sì, andiamo! Pronti a partire.
Sabine: Uffa, che traffico! Prendi un'altra strada, qui ci sono troppe macchine.
Pietro: Hai ragione, la strada per il mare è sempre trafficata. Portiamo pazienza!

Valigia – Suitcase

Teach Yourself Italian

La radio - Radio
Sulla spiaggia – On the beach
E dove la metto? – and where do I put it?
Dalla a me – give it to me.
Nel portabagagli – In the trunk
Metti un po' di musica – Put on music
Sì, andiamo – Yes, let's go
Pronti a partire – ready to go
Uffa, che traffico – uff, what a traffic
Un'altra strada – another street
Troppe macchine – too many cars
Hai ragione – you are right
Il mare – the sea
Sempre trafficata – there is always too much traffic
Portiamo pazienza – let us be patients

Grammar

Imperative with Tu-Noi-Voi

The *tu* and *voi* forms are identical to their corresponding present indicative forms, except for the *tu* form of *-Are* verbs, which add *-a* to the root. *domandare - domanda.*

The *noi* form corresponds to the English "**Let's...**" and also mimics the present subjunctive form - but is identical to the common present indicative.

Andiamo – Let's go

Vediamo – Let's see

Parlare	Scrivere	Partire	Finire
Tu Parl*a*	Scriv*i*	Part*i*	Finisc*i*
Noi Parl*iamo*	Scriv*iamo*	Part*iamo*	Fin*iamo*
Voi Parl*ate*	Scriv*ete*	Part*ite*	Fin*ite*

Remarks: When using the imperative form in negative for Tu, the verb remains in infinitive.

Non parlare *- Don't speak*

Non Scrivere *- Don't write*

Teach Yourself Italian

Non Partire - Don't go

Non Finire - Don't finish

Some irregular verbs in the imperative tense.

Andare – Go

Va (vai – va')
Non andare

| (Non) | Vada
Andiamo
Andate
Vadano | a
scuola |

Venire - Come

Vieni
Non venire

| (Non) | Venga
Veniamo
Venite
Vengano | a casa
dopo
domani |

Vai con lui – go with him
Vieni con me – come with me
Non andare con me – don't come with me

Avere – Have

Abbi
Non avere

Essere – Be

Sii
Non essere

Impaziente

	Abbia	Fretta		Sia	
(Non)	Abbiamo		(Non)	Siamo	Impazienti
	Abbiate			Siate	
	Abbiano			Siano	

Non abbiamo Fretta – Let's not be in a hurry

Non essere impaziente – Don't be impatient

Dare – Give

Stare – Be

*Da' (Dai / Da')
Non dare

Sta (Stai / Sta')
Non stare

	Dia	La		Stia	Fermo
(Non)	Diamo	precedenza	(Non)	Stiamo	
	Date			State	Immobili
	Diano			Stiano	

Date la precedenza – Give the priority

Stia fermo – Be still

Stiamo immobili – Let's be still

* Remarks: Be careful with the accent, Dà is the third singular person of the present tense.

Fare – Do / Make

Dire – Say / Tell

Fa (Fai / Fa')
Non fare

Di'
Non dire

bugie

Teach Yourself Italian

	Faccia	silenzio		Dica
(Non)	Facciamo		(Non)	Dicciamo
	Fate			Dite
	Faccinio			Dicano

Fa' silenzio – be silent
Non dica bugie – don't lie

Special Cases

Due to their spelling the verbs Dare –Dire – Fare have a peculiarity with the pronouns.

Dare - Give
Dammi una penna, **dammela** subito per favore– Give me a pen, give it to me immediately, please.
Dammene almeno uno, per piacere. – Give me at least one, please.
Dacci dei soldi, fratello, **Dacceli**, ti preghiamo, **Daccene** molti. – Give us some money, brother, give it to us, we beg you, give us a lot.

Dire – Say / Tell
Dimmi la verità, **dimmela**, per piacere. – Tell me the truth, say it, please.
Dilla solo a me – Tell it to me only.

Dicci come stanno le cose! – Tell us how things are.
Ecco Pietro, **digli** tutto. – Here you are Pietro, tell them (tell him) everything.

Fare – Do / Make
Fammi un favore, **fammelo** ti prego, non dirmi di no. – Do me a favour, I beg you, don't tell me no.

Remarks: Andare – Go and Stare – Be are used as Dare, Dire and Fare. When they are followed by the infinitive, the pronouns are changeable.

Stammi a sentire o **sta'** a sentirmi! - Listen to me
Vaglielo a dire o **va'** a dirglielo. – Go and tell them (him).

Pay close attention to the verb Andarsene – Go away / Leave.

Vattene, non voglio ripeterlo. – Go away, I don't want to repeat it.
Non **andartene**, ti prego. – Don't go, I beg you.
(Non) **se ne vada** – Don't go (Polite speaking)
(Non) **Andiamocene** – Let's not go.

Teach Yourself Italian

(Non) **Andatevene** – Don't go away (you plural)

(Non) **Se ne vadano.** – Don't leave – go away (to them)

Vocabulary

Segnali-Avvisi - Signs

Affitto non ammobiliato	For rent, not furnished
Uscita	Exit
Pericolo	Danger
Entrata	Entrance
Proprietà privata	Private Property
Esaurito	Exhausted
Partenza	Departure
Avanti	Ahead
Attenti al cane	Be aware of the dog
Benvenuti	Welcome

Arrivo	Arrival
Silenzio	Silence
Divieto di accesso	Access not allowed
Alt	Stop
Rallentare	Slow down

Teach Yourself Italian
UNIT 16

Che Numero Porta? – What's your size?

In this UNIT you will learn:

- ❖ Subjunctive tense of verbs, relative pronouns
- ❖ Different vocabulary to be able to go to the doctor, to the pharmacy, to express one's health conditions

Che Numero Porta?

Giovane: Mi scusi signora, che numero porta?
Signora: Quaranta, pianta larga. Può prendermi per favore il modello che è in vetrina?
Giovane: Subito signora. La scarpa che ha scelto le permetterà di fare tanti chilometri senza stancarsi. Lei acquista una scarpa alla quale non manca davvero nulla.

> *Pianta larga – Large Sole*
> *Il modello – The model*
> *Vetrina – Shop window*

Subito signora – Right now, Madam
Chilometri – Kilometers
Non manca davvero nulla – It really does not miss anything *(A shoe with all the best features.)*

Grammar

Relative Pronouns

Relative Pronouns substitute for the noun, connect two clauses. The clause introduced by the pronoun is subordinate and is dependent on the main clause.

The relative pronouns are: *Chi, Che, Cui,* and *Il quale.*

Che	=	il quale
		la quale
		i quali
		le quali

Accanto a me era seduto un ragazzo **che (il quale)** parlava da solo. – Next to me there was a boy sitting that talked to himself.

In centro ho conosciuto la mia fidanzata, **che (la quale)** sposerò. – Downtown I've met my girlfriend, whom I will marry.

Portami i bagagli **che (i quali)** sono sulla sedia. – Bring me the luggage that is on the chair.

Teach Yourself Italian

Mi piacciono le commedie di Pietro che (**le quali**) sono in scena in teatro. – I like Pietro's comedies, the ones that are stage at the theater.

		il quale
		la quale
Cui	=	i quali
		le quali

Non conosco il ragazzo **a cui** (**al quale**) hai prestato la moto. – I don't know the boy whom you lent the motorbike to.

Conosco la ragazza **con cui** (**con la quale**) stavi parlando. – I know the girl whom you were speaking to.

Ti dirò subito i motivi **per cui** (**per i quali**) non si può discutere. – I will tell you right away the reasons why it is not possible to argue.

Le persone **da cui** (**dalle quali**) vivo non sanno una parola d'italiano. – The people whom I live don't know a word in Italian.

		colui
Chi	=	colei
che		
		coloro
		le persone

Colui che dice questo sbaglia di grosso – Whoever says this, makes a big mistake.

Non puoi fidarti di (**chi** – **colui che** – **colei che** – **coloro che**) non conosci bene – You cannot trust people whom you don't know well.

Ciò che = quello che = quanto

È bello **ciò che** (**quello che** – **quanto**) hai fatto. – It's nice what you have done.

Remarks: With Colui / Colei the verb is in Singular.

Review Exercise

Complete with the correct relative pronoun

a) Chi è questa ragazza? (ho telefonato).
Questa è la ragazza alla quale ho telefonato.

b) Chi è quel signore? (ho spedito l'invito)
c) Chi sono quelle ragazze? (ho mandato le rose)

d) Chi sono quelle bambine? (ho regalato le caramelle)

e) Interessante quell'uomo! Chi? (parlavo prima)

Vocabulary:

L'abbigliamento – Clothing

Teach Yourself Italian

Per Uomini – For Men *Per Donne – For Women*

La giacca - Jacket		L'abito	Dress
I pantaloni - Trousers		La gonna	Skirt
Il cappello	Hat	La camicia	Blouse
Le scarpe - Shoes		Il busto	Bustier
I sandali	Sandals	Le calze	Socks
I mocassini - Moccasins		Le scarpe	Shoes
I lacci	Shoelaces	La giacchetta	Jacket
Il fazzoletto	Handkerchief	Il maglione	Pullover
La camicia	Shirt	Il cappellino	Cap
La maglia	T-shirt	I guanti	Gloves
I guanti	Gloves	La borsetta	Purse
La cintura	Belt	Il velo	Veil
Le bretelle	Straps		
I polsini	Cuffs		
La cravatta	Tie		
I calzini	Socks		

Farmacia - Drugstore

Vorrei un'aspirina - I would like an aspirine

Un lassativo - A laxative

Un calmante - A pain killer / sedative

Pastiglie per la tosse - Pills for the cough

Vorrei qualcosa per la dissenteria - I would like something for dysentery

Raffreddore - Cold

Cotone - Cotton

Benda - Bandage

Schiuma da barba - Shaving foam

Rasoi - Shavers

Fiala - Phial/Vial

Inalazione - Inhalation

Teach Yourself Italian

Infezione — Infection

Pomata — Ointment

Siringa — Syringe

Può controllarmi la pressione? - Can you monitor my blood pressure?

Medico - Doctor

Non mi sento bene - I don't feel well

Chiami un dottore - Call a doctor

Vorrei l'indirizzo di un dentista - I would need the address of a dentist

Ho dolori a — It hurts – I have pain

Devo restare a letto - I must (have to) stay in bed

Posso uscire? — Can I go out?

Cosa posso mangiare? - What can I eat?

Devo andare in ospedale - I should go to the hospital

Quanto le devo? - How much do I owe you?

Malattie - Diseases

Allergia	Allergy
Bronchite	Bronchitis
Emicrania	Migraine
Emorroidi	Haemorrhoids
Indigestione	Indigestion
Influenza	Flu
Reumatismi	Rheumatisms
Stitichezza	Constipation
Ulcera	Ulcer

Teach Yourself Italian

Sintomi - Symptoms

Affanno	Shortness of breath
Brividi	Chills
Capogiri	Dizziness
Crampi	Cramps
Febbre	Fever
Gonfiore	Swelling
Infiammazione	Inflamation
Insonnia	Insomnia

Mal di gola (mi fa male la gola) - Sore throat

Mal di testa (mi fa male la testa) - Headache

Italian Joke

Dal barbiere

Un mendicante entra, forse per la prima volta in vita sua, nel negozio di un barbiere. La barba!

Esclama, sono invitato al matrimonio di un collega. A rasatura terminata, il barbiere domanda: Vuole un poco di alcool? Beh, un goccio per gradire, bevo raramente al mattino...

Autore Anonimo.

Teach Yourself Italian
UNIT 17

Una Bella Ragazza – A beautiful girl

In this UNIT you will learn how:

- ❖ To speak in present subjunctive tense and its conjugations.
- ❖ To use the present perfect subjunctive and irregular verbs in this time.
- ❖ To use several useful terms such as: *Sport, Fishing, Tennis, Countries, Languages and Animals.*

Una Bella Ragazza

Daniel: Guarda che bella quella ragazza! Penso che sia italiana.
Pietro: Secondo me, dato che ha i capelli biondi e gli occhi azzurri, è più facile che sia tedesca.
Daniel: Ci siamo incrociati all'università ma non ci siamo parlati. Non credo che si ricordi di me.
Pietro: Può darsi che sia arrivata da poco e che non conosca molte persone, prova a fare amicizia con lei!

Daniel: Eh, prima è meglio che io comprenda la situazione. Può darsi che la inviti al bar!
Pietro: Magari! Ops!! Non la vedo più, temo che se ne sia andata!

> *Guarda – Look*
> *Che bella – How beautiful / What a beautiful.*
> *Quella ragazza – That Girl*
> *Penso che sia italiana – I think she's Italian*
> *Secondo me – In my opinion*
> *Dato che - Since*
> *I capelli biondi – Blond hair*
> *Gli occhi azzurri – Blue eyes*
> *Tedesca - German*
> *Ci siamo incrociati – We've crossed each other*
> *Può darsi – Maybe*
> *Che sia arrivata da poco – That she has come not long ago.*
> *Prova a fare amicizia con lei – Try to be her friend*
> *Prima - First*
> *È meglio che io comprenda – it is better if I understand*

Teach Yourself Italian

La situazione. – The situation

Magari! - Perhaps

Non la vedo più – I cannot longer see her

Temo che se ne sia andata - I'm afraid she's gone.

Grammar

Present Subjunctive Tense

It expresses doubt, possibility, uncertainty, personal feelings, emotion, desire, or suggestions. This time in English is rapidly becoming extinct, but in Italian, the subjunctive tense is alive and flourishing, both in speaking and writing.

The same conjugation is used for Io, tu, lui, lei, Lei in the three groups (Are, Ere, Ire).

Parl - are

Pietro pensa	Che	Io tu lui lei Lei	(non) parli	l'inglese.

noi	parl**iamo**
Voi	parl**iate**
Loro	parl**ino**

Pietro pensa che Io parli L'inglese – Pietro thinks that I speak English.

Scriv - ere

Pietro vuole	Che	Io tu lui lei Lei	(non)	Scriv**a**	Un libro.
		Noi		Scriv**iamo**	
		Voi		Scriv**iate**	
		Loro		Scriv**ano**	

Pietro vuole che tu scriva un libro – Pietro wants that you write a book.

Part - ire

Io tu lui lei	(non)	part**a**	Fra cinque minuti.

Teach Yourself Italian

Pietro crede Che Lei

noi	part**iamo**
Voi	part**iate**
Loro	Part**ano**

* *The same conjugation is used for the second group -Ere and the third group -Ire.*

Pietro crede che partiamo fra cinque minuti –
Pietro thinks that we leave in five minutes.

Fin - ire

Pietro crede	che	Io / tu / lui / lei / Lei	(non)	finis**ca**	presto.
		noi		Fin**iamo**	
		Voi		Fin**iate**	
		Loro		Finis**cano**	

*Pay close attention to ISC suffix.

Phrases that call for the subjunctive tense include:

Credo che... - I believe that...

Suppongo che... - I suppose that...

Immagino che... - I imagine that...

È necessario che... - It is necessary that...

Mi piace che... - I'd like that...

Non vale la pena che... - It's not worth it that...

Non suggerisco che... - I'm not suggesting that...

Può darsi che... - It's possible that...

Penso che... - I think that...

Teach Yourself Italian

Non sono certo che... - I'm not sure that...

È probabile che... - It is probable that...

Ho l'impressione che... - I have the impression that...

Present Perfect Subjunctive

Pietro	Crede		lei **sia partita**
	Teme	Che	loro **siano uscite**
	Spera		Daniel **abbia perso** i soldi
			loro (non) **abbiano scritto**

Penso che lei sia partita – I think that she's gone.

The use of the subjunctive or the infinitive is linked to the subject; you can use the infinitive only if the subject is the same in the main and in the subordinate clauses.

> Io credo **che** tu **abbia** ragione – I believe that you are right.
> Tu credi **di avere** ragione – You think to be right.
> Io credo **che** lui **abbia** ragione – I think that he's right.

Lui crede **di avere** ragione. – He thinks he's right.

Irregular verbs in the Subjunctive

Essere – Be

Pietro crede	Che	Io tu lui lei Lei	(non)	**Sia**	In centro.
		noi		**Siamo**	
		Voi		**Siate**	
		Loro		**Siano**	

Pietro crede che io sia in centro – Pietro thinks that I am downtown.

Avere - Have

Pietro crede	che	Io tu lui lei Lei	(non)	**Abbia**	ragione.
		noi		**Abbiamo**	
		Voi		**Abbiate**	

Teach Yourself Italian

Loro **Abbiano**

Pietro crede che noi abbiamo ragione – Pietro thinks that we are right.

Stare – Be

| Spera | Che | io **stia**
tu **stia**
lui / lei **stia**
noi **stiamo**
voi **stiate**
loro **stiano** | Bene |

Dare

| (non) è bene | che | io **dia**
tu **dia**
lui / lei **dia**
noi **diamo**
voi **diate**
loro **diano** | i soldi per sprecare. |

Andare

| Bisogna | Che | io **vada**
tu **vada**
lui / lei **vada**
noi **andiamo**
voi **andiate**
loro **vadano** | a scuola a studiare. |

Venire

		io **venga**	
		tu **venga**	
Spera	Che	lui / lei **venga**	a casa.
		noi **veniamo**	
		voi **veniate**	
		loro **vengano**	

Dire

		io **dica**	
		tu **dica**	
Vuole	Che	lui / lei **dica**	la verità
		noi **diciamo**	
		voi **diciate**	
		loro **dicano**	

Fare

		io **faccia**	
		tu **faccia**	
Desidera	che	lui / lei **faccia**	Silenzio.
		noi **facciamo**	
		voi **facciate**	
		loro **facciano**	

Dovere

		io **debba**	
		tu **debba**	
Penso	che	lui / lei **debba**	uscire questa sera.
		noi **dobbiamo**	
		voi **dobbiate**	
		loro	

Teach Yourself Italian
debbano

Potere

Spera/Spero	Che	io **possa** tu **possa** lui / lei **possa** noi **possiamo** voi **possiate** loro **possano**	fare quello che vuoi/vuole.

Volere

Pensa	Che	io **voglia** tu **voglia** lui / lei **voglia** noi **vogliamo** voi **vogliate** loro **vogliano**	lavorare ancora.

Togliere

Vuole		che	io **tolga** tu **tolga** lui / lei **tolga** noi **togliamo** voi **togliate** loro **tolgano**	il dente

Tenere

		io **tenga**	
		tu **tenga**	
Vuole	Che	lui / lei **tenga**	la casa in ordine.
		noi **teniamo**	
		voi **teniate**	
		loro **tengano**	

Uscire

		io **esca**	
		tu **esca**	
Perché non vuole	Che	lui / lei **esca**	questa sera?
		noi **usciamo**	
		voi **usciate**	
		loro **escano**	

Tradurre

		io **traduca**	
		tu **traduca**	
Desidera	che	lui / lei **traduca**	questo documento in inglese.
		noi **traduciamo**	
		voi **traduciate**	
		loro **traducano**	

You always use the Subjunctive after:

- ✓ Verbs indicating opinion, uncertain or personal affirmation (pensare, credere, supporre, ritenere, immaginare, parere, sembrare, può darsi, è facile – difficile, è possibile, è probabile – improbabile, si dice – dicono, si racconta – raccontano,

ecc.).
- ✓ Verbs or expressions of wish, fear, hope (volere, desiderare, preferire, augurarsi, sperare, temere, avere paura, ecc.).
- ✓ Verbs or expressions of judgement (bisogna, occorre, è necessario, urge, conviene, è meglio – peggio, è bene – male, è giusto – ingiusto, è naturale, è normale, è preferibile, è indispensabile, è logico – illogico, è strano, è importante, è pericoloso, è stupido, è incredibile, è un peccato, è una vergogna, ecc.).
- ✓ Verbs showing affection (essere lieto/a, essere felice, piacere, godere, dispiacere, rincrescere, rallegrarsi, essere spiacente, ecc.).
- ✓ Conjunctions (benchè, malgrado, sebbene, quantunque, nonostante, purchè, a patto che, a condizione che, senza che, prima che, nel caso che, supposto che, ecc.).

Remarks: Do not forget that all these verbs need to respond to a "Che".

Review Exercises

Complete with the Subjunctive. Use Penso che, Credo che, whenever needed.

a) Dove è la mamma? (in cucina) – **Credo che lei sia in cucina.**

b) Dove è il papà? (nello studio)

c) Dove sono le chiavi? (sul tavolo)

d) Ha fame? Sì, suppongo che _____.

e) Hanno nel portafoglio i soldi per fare la spesa? Sì, credo che _____.

f) Che cosa fa ora Daniela, cucina? Sì, penso che _____.

g) Che cosa fanno ora le cugine, guardano la TV? Sì, penso che _____.

h) Devo partire domani? Sì, voglio che _____ domani.

i) Dobbiamo uscire? Sì, voglio che _____ domani.

j) Capisce questa lingua? No, non credo che lui _____ questa lingua.

Teach Yourself Italian

k) Capiscono questa lingua? No, non credo che loro _____ questa lingua.

l) Vorremmo sapere la verità. Perché no, è meglio che voi _____ la verità.

m) È già arrivata Daniela? Temo che non _____ ancora arrivata.

n) Sono già arrivate a casa le signorine? È probabile che _____ già arrivate.

o) Pietro ha già finito quel lavoro? Non so, spero che l'_____ già finito.

Complete with the correct form of the Subjunctive

a) Pietro era in camera. (al bar) – **E tu pensavi che lui fosse al bar.**

b) I ragazzi erano in salotto. (in giardino) – E tu hai pensato che _____ in giardino.

c) Aveva paura? Sì, ma non pensavo che _____ tanta paura.

d) Avevano fame? Sì, ma non pensavo che _____ tanta fame.

e) Dovevi restare ancora. - Era opportuno che tu ____ ancora.

f) Dovevate studiare ancora. – Era meglio che voi ____ ancora.

g) Perché non gli hai scritto? – Perché pensavo che gli _____ tu.

h) Perché non le avete risposto? – Perché pensavamo che le _____ voi.

i) Finalmente sei venuto. – Perché, pensavi che io non _____?

j) Finalmente avete capito. – Perché, pensavi che noi non _____?

Vocabulary:

Sport

Vorrei noleggiare   - I would like to rent

Qual è la tariffa all'ora? -   What's the rate per hour?

Teach Yourself Italian

Volete venire con me? - Would you like to come with me?

Andiamo a fare un bagno - Let's take a bath

Qual è il tuo sport preferito? - What's your favourite sport?

Atletica - Athletics

Automobilismo – Car racing

Baseball - Baseball

Biliardo - Pool

Calcio - Football

Campeggio - Camping

Canottaggio – Rowing

Ciclismo – Biking / Cycling

Corsa dei cavalli – Horse race

Golf

Hockey

Marcia – Foot race/Marathon

Motociclismo - Motorcycling

Nuoto - Swimming

Pallacanestro - Basketball

Pallavolo - Volleyball

Pattinaggio - Skating

Pesca - Fishing

Ping-pong – Table tennis

Pugilato – Boxing

Sci - Skiing

Tennis

Teach Yourself Italian

Pesca - Fishing

Amo - Hook

Esca - Bait

Filo – String

Fucile subacqueo – Spear gun / Scuba gun

Galleggiante - Floating

Tennis

Giocare a tennis – Play tennis

Racchetta - Racket

Campo da tennis – Tennis field

Rete - Net

Righe – Lines

Gioco - Game

Servizio – Service

Fallo - Fault

Partita - Match

Paesi – Countries   *Lingue – Languages*

Argentina	Argentina	Arabo	Arabic
Australia	Australia	Cinese	Chinese
Belgio	Belgium	Francese	French
Brasile	Brazil	Giapponese	Japanese
Canada	Canada	Greco	Greek
Cina	China	Inglese	English
Egitto	Egypt	Portoghese	Portuguese
Francia	France	Russo	Russian
Germania	Germany	Spagnolo	Spanish
Giappone	Japan	Tedesco	German
Grecia	Greece	Turco	Turkish
Italia	Italy		
Messico	Mexico		
Olanda	Holland		
Palestina	Palestine		
Perù	Peru		

Teach Yourself Italian

Portogallo	Portugal
Regno Unito	UK
Russia	Russia
Spagna	Spain
Stati Uniti	USA
Sudafrica	South Africa
Svezia	Sweden
Svizzera	Switzerland
Turchia	Turkey
Ungheria	Hungary

Animali - Animals

Asino – Donkey

Cane - Dog

Cavallo – Horse

Bue – Ox

Coniglio - Rabbit

Gallo - Rooster

Corvo - Crow

Gallina – Hen

Gatto – Cat

Leopardo - Leopard

Oca - Goose

Tacchino - Turkey

Aquila - Eagle

Elefante - Elephant

Ippopotamo – Hippopotamus

Leone – Lion

Orso – Bear

Pappagallo - Parrot

Tigre – Tiger

Volpe - Fox

Uccelli – Birds

Teach Yourself Italian
Lupo - Wolf

UNIT 18

Un Capolavoro – A Masterpiece

In this UNIT you will learn:

- ❖ To speak in past perfect subjunctive form, conjugations of regular and irregular verbs.
- ❖ The use of time expressions, human body, greetings and general phrases.

Un Capolavoro

Mio fratello dice di essere un artista, ma non posso dire che sia vero, perché si è chiuso a chiave in camera sua, in modo che io e la mamma non lo guardassimo. Io pensavo che avrebbe fatto un quadro mediocre, temevo proprio che facesse un disastro. Alla fine lui è uscito dalla sua camera. Io non riuscivo a capire che cosa avesse disegnato... volevo buttare la sua opera prima che qualcuno la vedesse. Ma poi viene il bello...lo ha addirittura venduto!

Teach Yourself Italian

Un artista – An Artist
Che sia vero – That it is true
Camera sua – His bedroom
Quadro mediocre – Poor picture
Fare un Disastro – Set everything up for failure
Non riuscivo a capire – I could not understand
Volevo buttare – I wanted to throw out
La sua opera – His work
Ma poi viene il bello – but then comes the fun
Lo ha addirittura venduto – he even sold it.

Grammar

Past Perfect Subjunctive

It is a verbal form used to describe a fact considered not real or not objective, and distinguished by temporal anteriority with respect to an event that took place in the past. It can also be used in the hypothetical period of unreality when referencing the past.

Past Perfect Subjunctive of regular and irregular verbs is formed as follows:

Pensava	Parla	ssi	Bene	Parlare
	Legge		Molto	Leggere
Ha pensato	Capi	ssi	Tutto	Capire
	Parti		in aéreo	Partire
Voleva	Fo	sse	a casa alle 7	Essere
	Dice	ssimo	la verità	Dire
Desiderava	De		l'esame di medicina	Dare
		ste		
		ssero		
Credeva	Face		tutto il possibile	Fare
	Ste		Fuori	Stare
	Pone		in ordine i libri	Porre
	traduce		la lettera	Tradurre
	promuove		Tutti	Promuovere
	compi		una buona azione	Compiere

(with **che** between Desiderava and De)

Teach Yourself Italian

Beve	solo birra	Bere
Ave	Ragione	Avere

Pensavo che lei **fosse** a scuola e **avesse** molte cose da fare – I thought that she was at school and had many things to do.

Ho creduto che tutti **avessero capito** la spiegazione – I believed that everyone had understood the explanation.

Volevo che lei **fosse** la prima a sapere la notizia – I wanted her to be the first to hear the news.

Poteva darsi che non **avesse ricevuto** il mio messaggio – It could be that he had not received the message.

Vocabulary:

L'ora – The time

Che ora è?*	What time is it?
Che ore sono?	What time is it?
Sono le ore quindici	It is 3 pm.
È l'una (o'clock).	It is one
Sono le 3:15	It is 3:15
È l'una e un quarto	It's a quarter past one
È l'una e mezza	It's half past one
Sono le due meno un quarto	It is a quarter to two
Manca un quarto alle due	It's a quarter before two
Sono le ore ventiquattro	It is midnight
È mezzanotte	It is midnight

Teach Yourself Italian

Sono le ore dodici	It is twelve o'clock
È mezzogiorno	It's midday
Minuto	Minute
Secondo	Second
Ora	Hour
Giorno	Day
Notte	Night
Settimana	Week
Mese	Month
Anno	Year
Settimanale	Weekly
Quindicinale	Biweekly
Mensile	Monthly

In Italian there are two ways to ask for the time, the singular form when you believe it is anywhere from 12:01 to 12:59 and the plural form for anytime; however, in speaking Italian you can use the singular form at any time of the day.

Corpo Umano – Human Body

Gengiva - Gum

Gamba - Leg

Fronte - Forehead

Fianchi - Hips

Faccia - Face

Dita - Fingers

Dente - Teeth

Cuore - Heart

Cranio - Skull

Costola - Rib

Teach Yourself Italian

Collo - Neck

Natica - Buttock

Occhio - Eye

Orecchio - Ear

Petto - Chest

Spalla - Shoulder

Cervello – Brain

Testa - Head

Capello - Hair

Braccio - Arm

Bocca - Mouth

Ginocchio - Knee

Gola – Throat

Gomito – Elbow

Labbro – Lip

Lingua - Tongue

Naso - Nose

Pene - Penis

Vagina - Vagina

Sangue – Blood

Schiena - Back

Stomaco - Stomach

Pancia - Belly

Convenevoli - Greetings

Buongiorno	Good Morning
Buon pomeriggio	Good Afternoon
Buonasera	Good Evening
Buonanotte	Good Night
Arrivederci	See you, Bye bye, goodbye.

Teach Yourself Italian

Addio	Goodbye / Farewell
Piacere	A pleasure
Sono lieto di conoscerla	Pleased to meet you
Sono felice di rivederla	I am happy to see you again
Le posso presentare mia moglie?	Can I introduce my wife to you?
Come sta?	How are you?
Bene, grazie	Fine, thanks.

Ecco il mio indirizzo - Here you have my address

Questo è il mio numero telefonico - This is my telephone number

Posso chiederle un favore?	Can I ask you a favour?
Mi scusi	Excuse me

Mi dispiace	I am sorry
Accetti le nostre condoglianze	Please accept our condolences
Tanti saluti a tutti	Greetings to everybody
Le facciamo molti auguri	We give you many wishes
L'aspettiamo in Italia	We'll wait for you in Italy
Quando avrò il piacere di rivederla?	When will I have the pleasure to see you again?
Sono spagnolo	I am Spanish
Qualcuno parla greco qui?	Does anyone speak Greek here?
Mi dispiace disturbarla	I am sorry to bother you
Capisco un po' d'italiano	I understand a little Italian

Teach Yourself Italian

Non ho capito	I did not understand
Può ripetere?	Can you repeat?
Come si scrive?	How do you write it?
Può scrivermelo?	Can you write it for me?
Come si dice in italiano?	How do you say it in Italian?
Me lo dica lettera per lettera	- Tell me letter by letter / Spell that, please
Ho soltanto soldi italiani	- I only have Italian money
Vorrei un giornale italiano	- I'd like an Italian newspaper
È tardi	It is late
È presto	It is early
Accendi la luce	Turn on the light
Spegni la luce	Turn off the light

Vorrei fare un bagno	I'd like to take a bath
Ho fame	I am hungry
Andiamo a mangiare	Let's go to eat
Ho sete	I am thirsty
Vorresti bere qualcosa?	Would you like something to drink?
Ho sonno	I am sleepy
Andiamo a dormire	Let's go to sleep
Ho freddo	I am cold
Sono stanco	I am tired
Andiamo al cinema (ciname)	Let's go to the movies
A passeggio	For a walk
Un attimo prego	A moment, please
Come state?	How are you (plural)?

Teach Yourself Italian

Benissimo	Very well
Meglio	Better
Non molto bene	Not very well
Non molto male	Not very bad
Mi fa piacere	I am glad
Dove andate?	Where are you going?
Da dove venite?	- Where are you coming from?
Come vi chiamate?	What's your name?
Che cosa volete?	- What do you want?
Che cosa cercate?	What are you looking for?
Venite qua	Come here
Aspettate un attimo	- Wait a moment
Va bene, d'accordo	It is ok, I agree
Non vi capisco	- I don't understand you

Non lo so	- I don't know
Non posso	- I cannot
Potete farmi un favore?	- Can you do me a favour?
Non mancherò	- I will not miss it
Figuratevi	Imagine
Vi ringrazio molto	- I thank you so much / a lot
Permettetemi	Allow me
Per piacere	Please
Per favore	Please
Scusate	Excuse me
Che peccato	What a pity
Sfortuna	Bad luck
Taci	Be silent!
Smettila	Stop!

Teach Yourself Italian

Spicciati	Hurry!
Suppongo	I guess
Sono sicuro	I am sure
A proposito	By the way
Lasciatemi in pace	Leave me alone
Vattene	Go away
Hai ragione	You are right
Hai torto	You are wrong
Ti sbagli	You're mistaken
Sei un tesoro	You're a treasure
Tanti auguri	Happy Birthday
Complimenti	Compliments
Congratulazioni	Congratulations
Tanti saluti	Lots of greetings
Un po'	A little

Un pochino	A few
Affatto	Nothing
Lo capisco un po'	I understand it a little
Ma non lo parlo	But I don't speak it
Come ha detto?	What did you say?

Frasi - Phrases

A vicenda	Mutually
A quattr'occhi	Eyes wide open / face to face
A tu per tu	Face to face
Alla diavola	The hard way
Alla buona	The easy way
A memoria	By heart
Alla fin fine	At the end
A lungo andare	At the long run

Teach Yourself Italian

Di primo acchito — At first sight

Di buona lena — In good will

Di male in peggio — Bad into worst

In fretta — In a hurry

In fretta e furia - In haste / To rush something

In un batter d'occhio — In a blink of an eye

In un sorso — In one sip

In carne e ossa - In the flesh / Flesh and blood.

Per niente — No way

Per sempre — Forever

Per amore o per forza - By love or force

Zitto zitto — Quietly

Più presto si fa, meglio è - The soonest, the better

Né più né meno - No more no less

Parlare del più e del meno - To chat

Tosto o tardi	Sooner or later
Dio mio	My goodness
Bada/attenzione	Watch out
Vuoi tacere?	Be quiet, please!
Guai a te	Woe to you
Quale fortuna	What a luck
Peccato	Pity
Volesse Dio	God's will
Infelice	Unfortunate

Teach Yourself Italian
UNIT 19

Me ne vado – *I am leaving*

In this UNIT you will learn:

- ❖ How to talk about hypothetical situations and make conditional sentences, adjective degrees.
- ❖ Recognize different professions and jobs.
- ❖ Adverbs of manner, place, quantity, affirmation, negation.

Me ne vado

Marito: Così tu pensi che se io non ci fossi, tu avresti più fortuna?
Moglie: Sì, ho la sensazione che tu mi porti sfortuna.
Marito: Ho capito: me ne vado.
　　　　　(-------- Il giorno dopo-----)
Marito: Allora, come è andata senza di me? Ero io a portarti sfortuna?
Moglie: Vorrei che tu mi scusassi per ieri, ho esagerato.

Marito: Lascia perdere, non importa! Se non ti avessi ascoltato, non saresti uscito e non ti avrei comprato questo regalo!

Moglie: Oh, grazie amore mio, questo bracciale è stupendo! Magari ti avessi mandato via prima!

>Così – So
>
>Se io non ci fossi – If I were not here
>
>Più fortuna – more luck
>
>Ho la sensazione – I have the feeling
>
>Mi porti sfortuna – bring me bad luck
>
>Allora – So
>
>Senza di me – without me
>
>Ero io a portarti sfortuna? - Was I the one bringing you bad luck?
>
>Lascia perdere – Forget it
>
>Non importa – It doesn't matter
>
>Questo bracciale è stupendo – This bracelet is wonderful
>
>Magari ti avessi mandato via prima – I wish I had to kick you out before!

Grammar
Hypothetical Period
It is unreality when referencing the past.

Teach Yourself Italian

We can see it in different cases or scenes using If:

Se	**verrai,** non te ne **pentirai.**
	vieni con noi, **siamo** contenti.
	dici questo, sbagli.
	potranno, ti **aiuteranno.**

The condition is real. The consequence is sure, necessary. Sometimes in the consequences you can find an imperative.

Se vieni, avvertimi – If you come, let me know.

Se verrai, non te ne pentirai – If you come, you will not regret it.

Se vieni con noi, siamo contenti – If you come with us, we'll be happy.

Se dici questo, sbagli – If you say so, you are mistaken.

Se	**cambiassi** lavoro, **guadagnerei** di più.
	venissi con te, **avrei** più fortuna.
	prendessi questa medicina, ti **sentiresti** meglio.

The condition is uncertain, theorical, even possible as well as the consequence.

Se cambiassi lavoro, guadagnerei di più – If I'd change job, I'd earn more.

Se prendessi questa medicina, ti sentiresti meglio – If you'd take this medicine, you'd feel better.

Se
fossi ricco, **farei** il giro del mondo.
tu **avessi** preso quella medicina, **saresti** guarito.
conoscessi più lingue, tutto **sarebbe** più facile.

The condition is uncertain as well as the consequence.

Se fossi ricco, farei il giro del mondo – If I were rich, I would travel the world.

Se conoscessi più lingue, tutto sarebbe più facile – If I'd know more languages, everything would be easier.

Review Exercise

Complete with the correct form using the Hypothetical Period.

a) Rimarrai ancora? – Se potrò, _____ certamente.

b) Vorresti che Nicoletta venisse? – Sì, ____ contento, se Nicoletta _____.

c) Vorreste che Nicoletta prendesse marito? Sì, ___ contenti, se Nicoletta _____ marito.

d) Vorresti venire al concerto? – Magari _____ venirci (potere).

e) Vorreste venire anche voi al concerto? – Magari _____ venirci (potere).

f) Conosci quella ragazza? – Magari la _____ (conoscere).

Vocabulary

Mestieri e Professioni – *Crafts and Professions*

Il calzolaio fa e ripara le scarpe – The shoemaker makes and repairs shoes.

Il falegname lavora il legno – The carpenter works the wood.

Il muratore costruisce e ripara le case – The bricklayer builds and repairs houses.

Il fabbroferraio lavora il ferro – The blacksmith works iron.

L'orologiaio ripara gli orologi – The watchmaker repairs watches.

Il sarto cuce i vestiti – The tailor sews clothes.

L'idraulico monta l'impianto delle tubature dell'acqua e ripara le tubature e i rubinetti – The plumber installs the water pipes system and repairs the pipes and taps.

L'elettricista fa l'impianto dell'illuminazione e ripara i guasti dei fili e degli apparecchi elettrici – The electrician installs the electrical system and repairs the malfunctions of wires and electrical appliances.

Il mobiliere ripara e costruisce i mobili – The furniture maker repairs and builds furnishings.

Teach Yourself Italian

Il tappezziere ripara le sedie, le poltrone e i divani – The upholsterer repairs chairs, armchairs and sofas.

Il verniciatore pulisce e vernicia i mobili, le porte, le finestre e gli infissi – The varnisher cleans and paints furniture, doors, windows and frames.

L'avvocato difende le cause – The lawyer defends the cases.

Il medico cura gli ammalati – The doctor heals sick people.

Il chirurgo interviene nei casi gravi e opera – The surgeon intervenes in severe cases and operates.

Il notaio redige gli atti – The notary redacts / edits the acts.

L'ingegnere prepara il progetto della costruzione e ne dirige i lavori – The engineer prepares construction's project and directs the works.

Il maestro insegna nelle scuole elementari – The teacher teaches at elementary school.

Il professore insegna nelle scuole superiori – The professor teaches at high school.

Il pittore dipinge – The painter paints.

Lo scultore scolpisce – The sculptor carves.

L'architetto progetta e disegna – The architect plans and designs.

L'incisore incide – The engraver engraves.

Lo scrittore scrive – The writer writes.

Il poeta compone – The poet composes.

L'artista crea – The artist creates.

Teach Yourself Italian

Espressioni - *Expressions*

Dire di sì	Say yes
Dire di no	Say no
Credere di sì	Believe (yes)
Credere di no	Believe (no)
Essere in forse	Have doubts

Esclamazioni - *Exclamations*

Vattene - Get out

Perbacco - Gosh

Per Dio - For God's sake

Caspita - Good heavens

Accidenti – Damn

Accipicchia - Gee

Coraggio – (Bon) Courage!

Aiuto - Help

Piaccia a Dio - Please God

Che peccato - What a pity/shame

Mannaggia – Damn it

Magari – Maybe

Beato te – Lucky you

                    Povero me – Poor me

Teach Yourself Italian
UNIT 20

Ricchi Sfondati – Filthy Rich

In this UNIT you will learn:

❖ The use of Italian adjectives and several uses of Italian adverbs

Ricchi sfondati

Daniel: Ieri mi sono fidanzato con Chiara, siamo innamoratissimi. Io sono più giovane di lei di quindici anni, ma la differenza di età non conta. Lei ha un'ottima posizione, è un membro della ricchissima famiglia degli Stagi.
Pietro: Aaaahhh! Adesso capisco questa decisione tanto improvvisa quanto sorprendente, l'amore è la cosa più importante! E quando vi sposerete?
Daniel: Prestissimo, prestissimo.
Pietro: Bene! Tantissimi auguri.

> Innamoratissimi – so in love
> Più giovane di lei – younger than her
> Differenza – difference

Non conta – doesn't matter
Un'ottima posizione – Great financial status
Ricchissima famiglia – Very rich family
Tanto improvvisa quanto sorprendente - So sudden and surprising
Prestissimo – very, very soon
Tantissimi auguri – lots of wishes

Grammar

Italian Adjectives

There are three types of degrees: positive, comparative and superlative.

Positive Adjectives do not provide any comparison:

Il clima è bello – The weather is beautiful.

La poltrona è grande – The armchair is big.

Teach Yourself Italian

An adjective is comparative when expressing a comparison between people, animals, things, different degrees of quality, or diverse actions.

Comparative

Expressed by the correlative adverbs **tanto…quanto, così…come**:

Lui è **tanto** gentile **quanto** suo fratello – He is as gentle as his brother.

Lui è **così** intelligente **come** me – He is as intelligent as me.

Di Maggioranza - Comparative

Expressed by the adverb **più** (placed before the adjective) and the preposition **di** or the conjunction **che** (placed before the second term of comparison).

Sono **più** alto **di** lui - I am taller than him.

La mia casa è **più** grande **della** tua – My house is bigger than yours.

Il suo lavoro è **più** interessante **del** mio – His work is more interesting than mine.

Di minoranza – Comparative

Expressed by the adverb **meno** (placed before the adjective) and the preposition **di** or the conjunction **che** (placed before the second term of comparison).

Lei è **meno** difficile **di** quanto tu creda – She is less difficult than you think.
La mia casa è **meno** comoda **della** tua – My house is less comfortable than yours.

You use **Più... Che** – more than or **Meno...Che** – less than in the following cases:

Teach Yourself Italian
Between two adjectives of qualities

Quel ragazzo è **più** simpatico **che** bello – That boy is nicer than handsome.

La mia casa è **più** grande **che** comoda – My house is bigger than comfortable.

Between two quantities or nouns

Ho letto **più** romanzi **che** novelle – I've read more novels than short tales.

Qui sembrano esserci **più** macchine **che** persone – There seem to be more cars than people.

Between two actions or verbs

È **più** facile obbedire **che** comandare – It's easier to obey than to command.

È **più** difficile scrivere **che** parlare una lingua – It's more difficult to write than to speak a language.

Between nouns before prepositions

Viaggio **più** volentieri in aereo **che** in treno – I travel more willingly by airplane than by train.

Mi piace **più** stare a casa **che** uscire la sera – I like more to stay home than going out at night.

Between two adverbs

Agisce più istintivamente **che** razionalmente – He acts more instinctively than rationally.

Meglio tardi **che** mai – Better later than never.

Relative Superlative

It indicates an exceptional or extraordinary quality. It is formed using comparative with a definite article and placing a term such as **di, tra,** or **che** before the second term of comparison.

È la persona **più** simpatica che io conosca – He/she is the funniest person I've ever known.

Teach Yourself Italian

È stato il ragazzo **meno** spiritoso della compagnia – He was the less humorous boy from the group.

È il film **più** bello che io abbia mai visto – It is the nicest film I've ever seen.

Absolute Superlative

It offers no comparison with other people or things or qualities. It is formed by adding the ending -**issimo** to the adjective.

Io sono puntual**issimo** - I am very punctual

Tu sei ricch**issimo** - You are very rich

Maria è bell**issima** - Maria is very beautiful

Carmen è simpat**icissima** - Carmen is very funny

Loro sono ricch**issimi** - They are very rich

Loro sono bell**issime** - They are very beautiful

Irregular Comparatives and Superlatives

Positiv	*Comparative*	*Relative*	*Absolute Superlative*

	Comparativo	Superlativo relativo	Superlativo assoluto
Buono	Più buono/Migliore	Il più buono/Il migliore	Buonissimo/Ottimo
Cattivo	Più cattivo/Peggiore	Il più cattivo/Il peggiore	Pessimo
Grande	Più grande/Maggiore	Il più grande/Il maggiore	Massimo
Piccolo	Più piccolo/Minore	Il più piccolo/Il minore	Minimo
Bene	Meglio		Ottimamente/Benissimo
Male	Peggio		Malissimo
Molto	Più		Moltissimo
Poco	Meno		Pochissimo

Remarks:

Absolute Superlative can also be formed with:

✓ The prefixes: super, sopra, ultra, stra, arci.

È ultramoderno – It is ultramodern

Sei arcicontenta – You are super happy

Il gelato è strabuono – The ice cream is extra delicious

Teach Yourself Italian

Questo vino è sopraffino – This wine is the finest

Io sono superfortunato – I am super luckySome adjectives by repeating them.

Questo problema è facile facile – This problem is super easy

- ✓ Some expressions with Absolute Superlative.

Ricco sfondato – Filthy Rich

Stanco morto – Tired to death

Pieno zeppo – Completely full

Innamorato cotto – Madly in love

Bagnato fradicio – Soaking wet

Avverbi - *Adverbs*

Modify a verb, an adjective or another adverb. In English, adverbs are often formed by adding the suffix -ly to adjectives: slowly, softly, surely. Adverbs often answer the question *come* – how , *quando* – when , or *dove* – where.

Gli Avverbi di luogo che rispondono alla domanda Dove - *Adverbs of place answering to Dove.*

Quassù – Up here

Quaggiù – Down here

Lassù – Up there

Laggiù – Down there

Di qua - From here

Di là – From there

Al di là – Beyond

Dappertutto – All over

Per ogni dove – Everywhere

Daccapo – From the beginning

A destra – To the right

A sinistra – To the left

Tutt'intorno – All around

Teach Yourself Italian

Avanti - Forward

Di dove/Da dove – From where

Altrove - Elsewhere

Qui vicino – Here nearby

In disparte - Apart

Al lato/Accanto – Next

In nessun posto - Nowhere

- ❖ ***Avverbi Affermativi-Negativi-Dubitativi***
    Affirmative – Negative and Doubt Adverbs

Sì - Yes

Sì, signore – Yes, Sir

Certo/Di certo - Certainly

Sicuro - Sure/ certain

Indubbiamente - Undoubtedly

Senza dubbio - No doubt

Sicuramente - Certainly

Davvero - Really

Certamente - Certainly

Precisamente - Precisely

Sì, naturalmente – Yes, naturally

No, Non - No

Nossignore - No, Sir

Niente affatto – Not at all

In nessun modo – By no means

Mai - Never

Neanche/Nemmeno/Neppure – Not even

Nemmeno per sogno – In your dreams / No way, forget it.

Teach Yourself Italian

Forse/Può darsi/Può essere/Chissà – Maybe, Perhaps

Possibilmente - Possibly

Probabilmente - Probably

Avverbi di quantità – *Adverbs of quantity*

Quanto – How much / How many

Circa/su per giù – More or less

Poco/Po' - Little

Ancora Più – Even more

Molto/Assai - Much

Alquanto – A certain amount

Tanto – Much

Affatto - Entirely

Troppo – Too much

Quasi/Pressoché – Almost

Oltremodo/estremamente – Exceedingly

Solo – Only

Solamente – Only

Altrettanto – As much

Soltanto – Only

Meno - Less

Abbastanza - Enough

Anche/Pure – Too – as well

Neanche/Neppure – Not even

Nulla/Niente - Nothing

Teach Yourself Italian

Avverbi di luogo più comuni – More common adverbs of place

Dove - Where

Qui – Here

Qua – Here

Là-Colà – There

Sopra – Above

Sotto - Under

Su/In alto – Up there

Giù/In basso - Down there

Davanti – Ahead

Dovunque - Wherever

Dietro – Behind

Lontano - Far

Presso - At

Vicino - Close

Fuori - Outside

Review Exercises

Complete with the correct form of the Adjective

a) Daniela e Nicoletta sono belle. – Ma Nicoletta è **più** bella **di** Daniela.

b) Pietro e Giovanni sono simpatici. – Ma, Giovanni è ____ simpatico __ Pietro.

c) Capire e parlare: che cosa è più facile? Capire è ___ facile __ parlare.

Obbedire o comandare: che cosa è più semplice?

Comandare è ___ semplice __ obbedire.

Teach Yourself Italian
UNIT 21

Niente di nuovo - *Nothing new*

In this UNIT you will:

- ❖ Learn to speak using simple past and past perfect.
- ❖ Learn passive form.
- ❖ Learn different vocabulary.
- ❖ Complete your study of Italian language.

Niente di nuovo

Marco: Ciao, Pietro! Che cosa mi racconti di bello?
Pietro: Ciao Marco! Ieri sono stato a una conferenza, e ho rivisto il nostro professore di filosofia del liceo.
Marco: Ah sì, che bello! Mi ricordo di quando gli parlammo la prima volta, eravamo così timidi.
Pietro: Infatti! E ti ricordi di quando lo incontrammo a teatro a quel concerto di musica classica? Non uscì finché non ebbe salutato tutti i membri dell'orchestra!

Marco: Sì, è vero! Tememmo che sarebbe rimasto chiuso lì dentro!
Pietro: Che risate ci facemmo!

> *Una conferenza – A conference*
> *Filosofia - Philosophy*
> *Liceo – High School*
> *Timidi – Shy*
> *Infatti – Indeed*
> *Concerto – Concert*
> *Lì dentro – inside there*
> *Musica classica – Classic Music*
> *Finché - Until*
> *Membri dell'orchestra – Members of the orchestra*
> *Che risate ci facemmo – What a laugh we had*

Grammar

The Remote Past Perfect refers to the historical past or to events that have happened in the distant past relative to the speaker.

- ✓ Verbs of the first Group -Are, just drop the infinitive ending and add one of these

Teach Yourself Italian

personal endings to the root: *-ai, -asti, -ò, -ammo, -aste, -arono*.

- ✓ Verbs of the second group -Ere, just drop the infinitive ending and add these personal endings to the root: *-ei, -esti, -é, -emmo, -este, -erono*. Note that many regular *-ere* verbs have an alternative form in the first person singular, third person singular, and third person plural forms.
- ✓ For third group verbs -Ire, just drop the infinitive ending and add these personal endings to the root: *-ii, -isti, -í, -immo, -iste, -irono*.

Andare – Go	Temere – Fear	Partire – Leave	Capire – Understand
And-**ai**	Tem-**ei (etti)**	Part-**ii**	Cap-**ii**
And-**asti**	Tem-**esti**	Part-**isti**	Cap-**isti**
And-**ò**	Tem-**è**	Part-**ì**	Cap-**ì**
And-**ammo**	Tem-**emmo**	Part-**immo**	Cap-**immo**
And-**aste**	Tem-**este**	Part-**iste**	Cap-**iste**

And-**arono**   Tem-**erono**   Part-**irono**   Cap-**irono**
             (ettero)

Bianca and**ò** in banca questa mattina – Bianca went to the bank this morning.

Irregular verbs in the Past Remote Tense

Essere – Be		Fare – Do / Make		Dire – Say / Tell	
Fui	Contento	**Feci**	un ottimo lavoro	**Dissi**	una bugia
Fosti		**Facesti**		**Dicesti**	
Fu		**Fece**		**Disse**	
Fummo		**Facemmo**		**Dicemmo**	
Foste		**Faceste**		**Diceste**	
Furono		**Fecero**		**Dissero**	

Bere – Drink		Dare – Give		Stare - Be	
Bevvi	vino	**Detti** (diedi)	buoni consigli	**Stetti**	in giro
Bevesti		**Desti**		**Stesti**	
Bevve		**Dette** (diede)		**Stette**	
Bevemmo		**Demmo**		**Stemmo**	
Beveste				**Steste**	
				Stettero	

Teach Yourself Italian

Bevvero   **Deste**
                     Dettero
                     (diedero)

Avere	**Ebb**		Fortuna	
Volere	**Voll**		Rimanere	
Sapere	**Sepp**		Tutto	
Vedere	**Vid**	-i	un bello spettacolo	
Venire	**Venn**		con l'autostop	quel giorno.
Prendere	**Pres**	-e	la decisione giusta	quella volta.
Mettere	**Mis**		tutto in ordine	
Tenere	**Tenn**		una conferenza	in quell'occasione.
Conoscere	**Conobb**	-ero	molta gente	
Rimanere	**Rimas**		a casa	
Chiedere	**Chies**		un prestito in banca	
Chiudere	**Chius**		la porta della cucina	

Vivere	**Viss**	una brutta esperienza
Rispondere	**Rispos**	a mezza bocca
Scrivere	**Scriss**	tutto nel diario
Leggere	**Less**	un libro interessante
Vincere	**Vins**	un terno al lotto
Perdere	**Pers**	conoscenza
Rendere	**Res**	il resto dei soldi
Piacere	**Piacqu**	a tutti
Decidere	**Decis**	di non fare niente
Ridere	**Ris**	a crepapelle

Fui contento – I was happy

Facesti un ottimo lavoro – You did a wonderful job

Dicemmo una bugia – We said a lie

Bevesti vino – You drank wine

Dettero buoni consigli – They gave good pieces of advice

Teach Yourself Italian

Stetti in giro – I was around.

Irregular verbs in the First and Third person of the singular, and in the Third person of the plural.

The following verbs are irregular in the First and Third person of the singular and in the Third person of the plural. For the other conjugations, you will use the regular form (Scrivere: scrissi, scrivesti, scrisse, scrivemmo, scriveste, scrissero).

Decisi di non fare niente in quell'occasione – I decided to do nothing in that occasion.

> Preterite Perfect Tense refers to events, experiences or facts that happened or were already completed before a point of reference in the past.

Le telefon**ai** quando **ebbi ricevuto** la notizia.

Se ne and**arono**	**ebbero salutato** tutti.
Che cosa fac**esti**	**fosti guarita** dalla febbre?

Past Remote Tense
Preterite Perfect Tense

Le telefonai quando ebbi ricevuto la notizia – I called her when I had received the news.
Se ne andarono quando ebbero salutato tutti – They left when they had greeted everyone.

Teach Yourself Italian

Avverbi di tempo – *Adverbs of time*

Adesso - Now

Oggi - Today

Oggigiorno - Nowadays

Ancora – Still

Quando – When

Forse – Maybe

Stasera – This evening / Tonight

Ieri – Yesterday

Ieri sera – Yesterday Evening

Avantieri / L'altro ieri - Day before yesterday

Domani - Tomorrow

Dopo domani – Day after tomorrow

Domani mattina - Tomorrow morning

Domattina – Tomorrow morning

Domani sera - Tomorrow evening

Una volta – One time / Once

Dopo – After

Un'ora fa – An hour ago

Un anno fa – A year ago

Un mese fa – A month ago

Un giorno fa – A day ago

Poco fa – A little ago

Tempo fa – Time ago

Ogni qualvolta - Everytime

La settimana prossima – Next week

L'anno prossimo – Next year

Allora - Then

Ormai – By now

Spesso - Often

Sempre - Always

Teach Yourself Italian

Talvolta – Sometimes

Al più tardi – At the latest

Intanto – Meanwhile

Mai più - Never

Spesse volte – Many times

Più volte – Several times

Sempre più – Always more

Subito dopo – Soon after

In anticipo   - Upfront

Di buon'ora – Early

All'improvviso – Suddenly

Nello stesso tempo – At the same time

Al più presto - As soon as possible

Di quando in quando – From time to time

Presto - Soon

Subito - Immediately

Tardi – Late

Già - Already

Mai – Never

Finora – Until now

Insieme – Together

Piuttosto - Rather

Forse - Maybe

Può darsi – Could be

Chissà che – Who knows

Casomai – Just in case

Review Exercise

Complete with the correct form of the verb in the Remote Past Tense.

Teach Yourself Italian

a) Chi inventò il telegrafo? (G. Marconi) – **G. Marconi inventò il telegrafo.**

b) Chi fondò Roma? (Romolo) –

c) Chi andò per primo sulla Luna? (N. Armstrong) –

d) Chi furono i primi astronomi? (i Babilonesi) –

e) Chi furono i primi matematici? (gli Arabi) -

f) Chi scrisse questa lettera a Maria? La _____ io.

g) Chi lo conobbe quando venne a Roma? Lo _____ loro.

Perché non finiste il corso? Non lo ____ perché non ci ___ possibile.

UNIT 22

La Guida Racconta – The travel guide says

In this UNIT you will learn:

- ❖ To use active and passive voice
- ❖ To use final vocabulary by completing your Italian language course.

La guida racconta

Questa camera sepolcrale è stata costruita con grosse pietre regolari e finora sono state ritrovate due sepolture. Dai materiali recuperati, questa sarebbe stata costruita in un arco di tempo molto lungo.

> *Camera sepolcrale – Burial chamber*
> *Grosse pietre regolari – Regular big stones*
> *Finora – Until now*
> *Sepolture - Graves*
> *In un arco di tempo – Over a period of time*
> *Molto lungo – very long*

Teach Yourself Italian

Grammar

		Spiega		
		ha spiegato		
		spiegava		
Il professore		aveva spiegato		la lezione
		Spiegò		
		ebbe spiegato		
		Spiegherà		
		avrà spiegato		
		spiegherebbe		
		avrebbe spiegato		
		spieghi		
Penso		abbia spiegato		
	Che	il	spiegasse	
Pensavo		professore	avesse spiegato	

Active Tense

We can see in the chart below how to form the Active Voice or Active Tense.

La lezione	è (viene)		spiegata	dal professore
	è stata			
	era (veniva)			
	era stata			
	fu (venne)			
	fu stata			
	sarà (verrà)			
	sarà stata			
	sarebbe (verrebbe)			
	sarebbe stata			
Penso			sia (venga)	
	che	la nuova lezione	sia stata	
Pensavo			fosse (venisse)	
			fosse stata	

Il professore **spiega la lezione** – The teacher explains the lesson.

Teach Yourself Italian

Pensavo che il professore avesse spiegato la lezione – I thought that the teacher had explained the lesson.

Passive Tense

It is formed by the auxiliary *Essere* followed by the past participle of the verb to be conjugated.

You can see in the chart below how to form the Passive Voice or Passive Tense.

La **lezione è spiegata dal professore** – The lesson is explained by the teacher.

Pensavo che la nuova lezione fosse stata spiegata dal professore – I thought that the new lesson had been explained by the teacher.

Review Exercise

Transform from Active Voice to Passive Voice

    a) Il medico ordina la cura – **La cura è stata ordinata dal medico.**

b) La guida illustra il monumento -
_____

c) Chi ha scritto la Divina Commedia? (D. Alighieri) _____

d) Tu devi fare questa ricerca -
_____

e) Stasera gli imprenditori concluderanno l'affare -
_____

f) La mamma racconta al bambino una favola -
_____
_____

Teach Yourself Italian

Vocabulary:

Congiunzioni - *Conjunctions*

Anzi   - In fact / Actually

Benché - Although

Affinché – So that

Qualora – In case/if

Siccome – How / Since

Però - But / However

Quindi – Therefore / Then

Perciò - Thus

Poiché - Because

Tranne – Except

Se – If

Ma - But

E – And

Ed – and (in front of vowels)

Che – What

Purché – As long as, provided that

Quando – When

Cioè – That is

Dunque – Therefore / So / Well

Mentre - While

Né – Neither

Oppure - Or

Teach Yourself Italian
Conclusion

*Grazie infinite di aver scelto per la vostra esperienza di studio Imparare **l'italiano Conversando del Dottor Yeral E. Ogando**. Fortunatamente siete arrivati alla fine del corso, e quindi siete pronti a parlare l'italiano con chiunque.*

*Vi incoraggio a continuare a esercitarvi e a parlare italiano in ogni momento, perchè, come ho già detto, **la pratica lo rende perfetto**. Visitate il nostro sito web per maggiori informazioni.*
   Dio vi benedica e ci vediamo la prossima volta.

Yeral Ogando
www.aprendeis.com

BONUS PAGE

Dear Reader,

You need to download the MP3 Audio files to follow this unique method gradually. Please visit our website at: http://aprendeis.com/italian--audio/

The username is "**italian**"

The password is "**italian2016**"

Just download the Zip File and you are ready to start your learning experience.

If you want to share your experience, comments or possible question, you may always reach me at info@aprendeis.com

Remember:

Reviews can be tough to come by these days, and you, the reader, have the power to make or break a book. If you have the time, share your review or comments with me.

Thank you so much for reading ***Teach Yourself Haitian Creole*** and for spending time with me.

In gratitude,

Teach Yourself Italian

Yeral E. Ogando

Yeral E. Ogando comes from a very humble origin and continues to be a humble servant of our Lord Almighty; understanding that we are nothing but vessels and the Lord who called us, also sends us to do His work, not our work. ***Luke 17:10 "So likewise ye,***

when ye shall have done all those things which are commanded you, say, We are unprofitable servants: we have done that which was our duty to do."

Mr. Ogando was born in the Caribbean, Dominican Republic. He is the beloved father of two beautiful girls "Yeiris & Tiffany"

Jesus brought him to His feet at the age of 16-17. Since then, he has served as Co-pastor, pastor, Bible School teacher, youth counselor, and church planter. He is currently serving as the Secretary for the Dominican Reformed Church as well as the liaison for Haiti and USA.

Fluent in several languages Mr. Ogando is the Creator and owner of an Online Translation Ministry operating since 2007; with Native Christian translators in more than 25 countries.

(www.christian-translation.com),

The most exciting thing about his Translation Ministry is that thousands of people are receiving the Word of God in their native language on a daily basis and hundreds of ministries are able to reach the world through the work of Christian-Translation.com along with his translation network of 17 websites in different languages related to Christian Translation.

Glossary of Verbs

A

Abilitare – Train
Abituare – Get used
Accarezzare – Caress
Assomigliare - Resemble
Assolvere - Absolve
Assicurare - Ensure
Aspettare - Wait
Ascoltare - Listen
Ascendere – Ascend
Arrostire - Roast
Approfondire - Deepen
Appendere - Hang
Apparire – Appear
Aggiustare - Adjust
Aggiungere - Add
Agevolare - Facilitate
Affittare - Rent
Adattare - Adapt
Accudire – Look after
Accorrere - Rush
Accoppiare - Match
Accertare - Determine
Affogare - Drown
Aggrinzire - Wrinkle
Allibire – Be left speechless
Ammattire – Go mad
Ammutolire – Fall silent
Andare - Go

Arrivare – Arrive
Asciugare – Dry
Assoldare – Engage
Attecchire – Take root (Essere e Avere)
Avanzare – Advance / Progress   (Essere e Avere)
Avvizzire – Wither
Accendere – Turn on
Accludere - Include
Accogliere - Welcome
Accrescere – Increase
Addurre – Adduce
Affiggere – Post
Affliggere – Afflict
Alludere – Allude
Ammettere - Admit
Apprendere – Learn
Aprire - Open
Ardere - Burn
Assalire – Assault
Assistere – Assist
Assumere – Hire
Avvolgere – Wrap
Acquistare – Acquire / Buy
Acconsentire - Consent
Arricchire – Enrich
Agire - Act

B

Bastare – Suffice
Bisognare - Need
Brillare - Shine   (Essere e Avere)

Benedire – Bless
Ballare - Dance
Bere – Drink
Bussare - Knock

C

Cadere – Fall
Cambiare - Change
Cessare - Cease   (Essere e Avere)
Circolare - Circulate (Essere e Avere)
Constare - Consist
Convenire – Agree (Essere)
Costare – Cost   (Essere e Avere)
Crescere – Grow up
Crollare - Collapse
Cedere – Surrender
Credere - Believe
Camminare – Walk
Cantare - Sing
Comprare – Buy
Chiedere - Ask
Chiudere – Close
Comprendere - Comprehend / Understand
Comprimere - Compress
Concedere - Grant
Concorrere – Concur
Condurre - Conduct
Conoscere – Know
Consumare - Consume
Contundere – Contuse
Convincere – Convince

Coprire – Cover
Correggere – Correct
Correre – Run
Corrompere - Corrupt
Costruire – Build/Construct
Costituire – Constitute
Cogliere – Take
Commettere - Commit
Comparire – Appear
Compiere -   Fulfill
Compire – Accomplish
Comporre – Compose
Cucinare - Cook

D

Decadere – Decay
Derivare - Derive
Deviare - Divert   (Essere e Avere)
Dimagrire – Lose weight
Diminuire – Decrease
Dipendere – Depend
Divenire – Become / Turn
Diventare – Become / Turn
Dolere - Ache (Essere e Avere)
Domandare - Ask
Durare – Last
Definire - Define
Dare – Give
Decidere - Decide
Decrescere – Decrease
Difendere - Defend
Dipingere – Paint

Dire – Say / Tell
Dirigere – Direct
Discendere - Descend
Discutere – Argue
Disporre – Dispose
Dissolvere – Dissolve
Dissuadere – Dissuade
Distinguere – Distinguish
Distruggere – Destroy
Dividere – Divide
Dolersi – Lament
Dovere – Must / Should / Owe

E

Emanare – Emanate
Entrare – Get in
Esistere – Exist
Evadere - Evade
Eccellere – Excel
Eleggere - Elect
Emergere – Emerge
Equivalere – Equal
Escludere – Exclude
Esigere – Require / Demand
Espellere – Expel
Esplodere – Explode
Esporre – Expose
Esprimere – Express
Estendere – Extend
Estinguere – Extinguish
Estrarre - Extract

F

Finire – Finish
Fuggire – Run away
Frenare – Brake
Fremere - Tremble
Fare – Do / Make
Fingere – Pretend
Fondere - Melt
Friggere - Fry

G

Giovare - Profit
Guarire – Heal
Gemere - Whine
Giungere – Reach
Godere - Enjoy

I

Imputridire - Rot
Incespicare – Stumble
Infiacchire – Weaken
Infuriare – Get angry
Insuperbire – Make arrogant / proud
Invecchiare – Get old
Illudere - Delude
Immergere – Immerse / Plunge
Imporre - Impose
Imprimere – Print / Impress
Incidere – Engrave / Record
Includere - Include
Indulgere – Indulge

Introdurre – Introduce
Invadere - Invade

L

Luccicare – Sparkle
Ledere - Damage
Leggere – Read
Lottare – Fight

M

Mancare – Miss / Lack
Maturare - Mature
Migliorare - Improve
Morire - Die
Maledire – Curse
Mettere – Put In
Mordere – Bite
Mungere - Milk
Muovere - Move
Mietere – Harvest

N

Nascere – Be born
Naufragare - Shipwreck (Essere e Avere)
Navigare - Navigate (Essere e Avere)
Nuocere – Harm
Nuotare – Swim
Notare – Note / Mark / Observe
Nascondere – Hide

O

Occorrere – Be required
Originare - Originate
Offrire – Offer

P

Parere - Seem
Partire - Leave
Peggiorare – Get worst
Perire - Perish
Piacere – Like
Progredire – Progress
Prosperare – Prosper
Percuotere – Strike
Perdere – Lose
Piangere – Cry
Piovere – Rain
Porgere – Give
Porre   - Put
Potere - Be able / Can
Prendere – Take
Presumere – Presume
Pretendere – Pretend
Prevenire – Prevent
Proteggere – Protect
Pungere – Sting

R

Rabbuiare – Darken
Restare – Stay
Rimanere – Remain
Rinascere – Revive / Be born again

Rincrescere – Regret
Ringiovanire - Rejuvenate
Risanare – Restore / Heal
Riparare – Repair / Fix
Risplendere - Shine (Essere e Avere)
Risultare – Result
Risuscitare – Resuscitate
Redimere – Redeem
Resistere – Resist
Ridere - Laugh
Ridurre – Reduce
Risolvere - Resolve
Rispondere – Respond / Answer
Rompere - Break
Rovinare – Ruin / Spoil
Ricevere - Receive
Ripetere – Repeat

S

Salire – Go up / Climb
Seguire – Continue / Proceed
Salpare - Sail (Essere e Avere)
Saltare - Jump (Essere e Avere)
Sbiadire – Fade
Sbigottire - Dismay
Scappare – Escape
Scivolare – Slip / Slide
Scoppiare – Burst / Explode
Sembrare - Seem
Sorgere – Arise / Spring
Sapere - Know

Sostare – Stop / Halt (Essere e Avere)
Spiacere - Displease
Scegliere – Choose / Select
Scendere – Go down
Scindere – Split / Divide
Scrivere - Write
Soddisfare – Satisfy
Scuotere - Shake
Spargere – Spread
Spegnere – Turn off
Spendere – Spend
Spingere - Push
Stare – Be
Stringere – Tighten / Squeeze
Svenire – Faint

T

Tacere - Be silent
Toccare – Touch
Tornare – Return / Come back
Tirare - Pull
Trascurare – Neglect
Trovare – Find

U

Uscire - Go out

V

Vacillare - Hesitate
Volare - Fly

Valere - Be worth
Venire - Come
Vivere - Live
Vendere - Sell
Vestire – Get dressed

Glossary of Words

A

Acqua - Water
Acquirente - Buyer
Acquedotto – Aqueduct

Acquerello – Watercolor

Acquitrino - Swamp

Acquisto – Acquisition

Atto – Act

Attore - Actor

Attuale – Current / Present

Affetto - Affection

Aspetto – Appearance

Assoluto - Absolute

Ammissione - Admission

Assurdo – Absurd / Ridiculous

Avverso – Adverse

Avversario – Adversary/Opponent

Accademia – Academy

Apparente – Apparent

Avviso - Notice / Warning

Affluente – Affluent / Tributary

Assalto - Assault

Allegoria – Allegory

Anniversario – Anniversary

Assunto – Recruit

Antenna – Antenna

Attento – Careful / Observant

Attitudine - Attitude

Azione - Action

Avarizia – Greed

Arazzo - Tapestry

Alunno – Pupil

Altero - Arrogant

Àmbito – Scope

Àncora - Anchor

Ancòra - Yet / Still

Acrobazie - Acrobatics

Aristocrazia – Aristocracy

Agenzia - Agency

Anemia - Anemia

Atmosfera - Atmosphere

Anestesia – Anesthesia

Autopsia - Autopsy

Autobus – Bus

Ateo - Atheist

Affare - Business

Anima - Soul

Aquila - Eagle

Aria - Air

Armonia – Harmony

Artista - Artist

B

Basso – Low / Small
Banca - Bank
Bambino – Little Boy / Child

Bello - Beautiful

Borsa – Purse

Bicchiere – Glass

Birra – Beer

Bosco – Woods

Branda - Cot

Brezza - Breeze

Baffi – Mustache

Burro - Butter

Brutto - Ugly

Bottone - Button

C

Cavallo – Horse
Cassa – Box / Cash register / Trunk
Caldo – Warm / Hot
Canzone – Song
Cappero – Caper
Calza - Sock
Caffè - Coffee
Capezzolo – Nipple
Cattivo – Evil
Chiodo – Nail
Cielo - Sky / Heaven
Città - City
Combustibile – Fuel
Comico - Funny
Consiglio – Advice
Consegna – Delivery
Console – Consul
Corruzione - Corruption
Collo - Neck
Cappello – Hat
Capello – Hair
Cappotto – Coat
Camino – Chimney
Casa - House
Caro – Expensive / Dear
Coppia – Couple

D

Dama – Lady
Danno - Damage
Decisione – Decision

Delega - Delegation

Dialetto – Dialect

Denuncia - Complaint

Dieta – Diet

Difesa - Defense

Difetto - Fault

Dio – God

Direzione - Direction

Disgusto – Disgust

Disordine – Disorder / Mess

Dono – Gift

Domanda - Question

E

Eccetera - Etcetera

Eccitante - Exciting

Economia – Economy

Edificio - Building

Elegante – Elegant

Elemosina – Alms / Charity / Donations

Energia – Energy

Episodio - Episode

Equipaggio - Crew

Eredità - Heritage

Esame - Exam

F
Fabbisogno - Requirement
Fabbrica - Factory
Facile – Easy

Facoltà - Faculty

Famelico – Starving / Hungry

Farina - Flour

Fatica – Fatigue

Favoloso - Fabulous

Favorevole - Favorable

Fede – Faith

Fedele – Faithful

Felice - Happy

Festa – Party

Fornaio – Baker

Forno – Furnace

Foro – Hole
Fortunato - Lucky

  Fotografia – Photo / Picture

Fretta - Hurry

Fumo – Smoke

Fuoco – Fire

G
Gelateria – Ice cream shop
Gelato - Ice cream
Geloso – Jealous
Generoso – Generous
Gentile – Gentle
Giardino – Garden
Gioia – Joy

Giornale - Newspaper

Giornalista – Journalist

Giorno - Day

Gita - Excursion

Giustizia - Justice

Gradevole – Pleasant

Gusto - Taste

Guardaroba – Wardrobe

Gota – Cheek

H

Hotel - Hotel

I

Idea - Idea

Ideale - Ideal

Igiene - Hygiene

Immagine - Image

Impiego - Employment

Impossibile - Impossible

Imprudente - Imprudent

Incontro - Encounter

Indumento – Garment

Inevitabile - Inevitable

Infelicità – Unhappiness

Innocenza – Innocence

Insalata – Salad

Insieme – Together

Insomma – In conclusion

Internazionale - International

Intervista – Interview

Intimità – Intimacy

Isola – Island

Istruttore - Instructor

L

Ladro – Thief
Lampone – Raspberry
Lattuga – Lettuce
Lavagna – Blackboard
Lavoro – Job / Work
Legge - Law
Legno - Wood

Limone - Lemon

Lingua – Language

Liquido – Liquid

M

Maccheroni – Macaroni

Macchina - Car

Macelleria – Butcher shop
Materasso - Mattress

Matita - Pencil

Melone - Melon

Mercato – Market

Mestiere – Craft / Profession

Mesto – Sad

Mondo - World

Museo - Museum

N

Naso – Nose

Natura - Nature

Necessità – Need / Necessity

Negozio – Shop / Store

Nervoso – Nervous

Noioso – Boring

Nostalgia – Homesickness

Nuovo - New

O

Occasione - Occasion

Odore - Odor

Oggi – Today

Ognuno – Each one

Ogni – Each

Olio – Oil

Ombra – Shadow

Opportunità – Opportunity

Originale – Original

Orologio – Clock / Watch

Ospite – Guest

Occhio – Eye

P

Pacco – Package
Paesaggio - Landscape
Paese – Country

Pagina - Page

Pane – Bread

Panetteria - Bakery

Parola - Word

Passaggio - Passage

Passeggero - Passenger
Passeggiata - Walk

Personale – Personal

Personalità – Personality

Pettine – Comb

Pezzo – Piece

Pigna – Pineapple

Pioggia – Rain

Pollo – Chicken

Porta – Door

Prossimo – Next

Q
Qualità – Quality

R
Reale - Real
Recente - Recent
Reddito – Income

Regina - Queen

Regola – Rule
Relazione – Relationship / Report

Responsabile – Responsible

Richiesta - Request

Riso – Rice

Risparmio – Saving

Rispetto – Respect

Ruota - Wheel / Tyre

S

Sacco – Bag / Sack
Salotto - Salon
Salute - Health

Sapore - Flavor

Saporito – Tasty

Seme – Seed

Sesso – Sex

Solitudine – Loneliness

Spesa – Expense

Spiaggia - Beach

Strada - Street

Succo - Juice

T

Taglio - Cut
Tasca - Pocket
Tavolo – Table

Testa – Head

Tristezza – Sadness

Troppo – Too much

Tutto - Everything

U

Udito – Hearing
Ufficio - Office
Uguale – Equal / Same

Uovo - Egg

Uscita - Exit

Utile - Useful

Urgenza – Urgency

V

Vacca - Cow
Valigia - Suitcase
Vegetale - Vegetable

Veloce - Fast / Quick

Velocità – Speed

Venuta – Arrival / Coming

Verità - Truth

Vuoto - Empty

Z

Zampa – Paw / Leg
Zuccheriera – Sugar bowl
Zanzara - Mosquito
Zucca - Pumpkin
Zona – Zone

Zucchero - Sugar

Zuppa - Soup

Zuppo - Wet

Other books written by Yeral E. Ogando

Printed in Great Britain
by Amazon